THE
PROPER WIT
OF POETRY

THE
PROPER WIT
OF POETRY

by

GEORGE WILLIAMSON

Tell me, O tell, what kind of thing is Wit,
Thou who Master art of it.
COWLEY

FABER AND FABER

24 Russell Square

London

First published in mcmlxi
by Faber and Faber Limited
24 Russell Square, London, W.C.1
Printed in Great Britain by
Western Printing Services Ltd., Bristol

For
JEHANNE
and
ALAN

CONTENTS

I

THE POET'S FEIGNING WIT

Stand close around, ye Stygian set,
  With Dirce in one boat convey'd!
Or Charon, seeing, may forget
  That he is old and she a shade.

LANDOR

For our time the wit of seventeenth-century poetry was first defined by T. S. Eliot. His tentative definition was later narrowed by F. R. Leavis to a 'line of wit' that extended to Pope. Although a modern concern, this is not a new topic of criticism. In Pope's time, moreover, the theory of poetic wit was reformulated by Addison—out of the explorations of Dryden. For their century the great 'wits' were Donne and Cowley, but our time often prefers a third. Marvell was not a wit for Addison, but in his prose satires he used and appreciated *The Rehearsal*, Etherege, Dryden, *Hudibras*, Donne, Rochester, and even 'Bishop Davenant' of *Gondibert*. And in poetry, we are inclined to think, his range of wit was exceeded by none. Yet the droll Marvell whom Dryden mentioned was the prose satirist.

But one thing must be said for Addison: he wrote before the tradition of wit was broken. In criticism the consequence of this break, for which Addison prepared the way, becomes clear when Hazlitt, in *The English Comic Writers*, defines wit and imagination as opposites: 'Imagination may be said to be the finding out something similar in things generally alike, or with like feelings attached to them; while wit principally aims at finding out something that seems the same, or amounts to a momentary deception where you least expected it, viz. in things totally opposite.' For Hazlitt the object of imagination is to magnify, of wit to diminish; and the purposes of wit are served by superficial resemblances between things generally unlike. The end of this course is reached in the doctrine of high seriousness, where Arnold, like Addison, separates force and wit in poetry. The seventeenth century made no such distinctions between wit and imagination, or their suggested rhetorical functions, but rather assimilated them to a perception of unexpected resemblances. When Addison called Wit 'a Resemblance and Congruity of Ideas', he had to make room for 'Surprize', and thereby suggested the potential conflict between surprise and congruity.

The common Elizabethan approach to poetry was rhetorical; for, as Bacon observed, there was no art of the imagination, but there was an art of language. The rhetorical forms as distinct from the grammatical forms of language were elaborately analysed and applied in the Renaissance. In poetry they often attained the status of a formal device. They were commonly taken as evidence of the poet's wit; they were at least a means of analysing its form. The most important art of poetry found in this time is Puttenham's, and it is divided into 'three Bookes: the first of Poets and Poesie, the second of Proportion' or prosody, 'the third of Ornament' or rhetorical figures. For Puttenham (I, iv) poetry is both 'musical speech' and 'figurative conveyance'. His *Arte of English Poesie*, after general considerations, settles down to Proportion and Ornament, or the principles of verse and figurative speech. Of its significance Sir John Harington remarked: 'where, as it were, a whole receit of Poetry is prescribed, with so many new named figures as would put me in great hope in this age to come would breed many excellent Poets'. When Fulke Greville spoke of imagination in

> Isis, *in whom the Poets feigning wit,*
> *Figures the Goddess of Authority,*

he defined its figurative function in the poet. Hence its product was commonly analysed by means of rhetoric into various kinds of rhetorical wit. It is this point of view that turns our attention to the significance of rhetorical devices in Renaissance poetry.

The first rule for making a poem, says George Gascoigne in *Certayne Notes of Instruction* (1575), is 'to ground it upon some fine invention'. He warns that 'what Theme soever you do take in hand, if you do handle it but *tanquam in oratione perpetua*, and never study for some depth of devise in the Invention, and some figures also in the handling thereof, it will appear to the skilfull Reader but a tale of a tub'. Later Sidney complained, in his *Defense of Poesy*, that few poems had any 'poetical sinews' or integration in them; for 'it will be found that one verse did but beget another, without ordering at the first what should be at the last; which becomes a confused mass of words, with a tingling sound of rhyme, barely accompanied with reason'. And Sidney did not tie the poet to Nature: 'so as hee goeth hand in hand with Nature, not inclosed within the narrow warrant of her guifts, but freely ranging onely within the Zodiack of his owne wit'.

To the force of Gascoigne's instruction the rhetorics bear ample witness. Puttenham's *Arte of English Poesie*, for example, is alert to the ways in which figures contribute to some depth of ingenuity in the invention. Furthermore, 'to study deeply for some fine devise' had a special force for a time in which some of the most ingenious forms of figurative expression were called 'devices'[1] and found their place in Puttenham's *Arte*. Bacon said, 'Emblem reduceth conceits intellectual to images sensible, which strike the memory more.' Puttenham emphasizes figurative conveyance as poetic dissimulation (III, vii) or 'ways seeking to inveigle and appassionate the mind'. In single words these ways begin with metaphor (xvii); in many words dissembling begins with allegory, 'the chief ringleader and captain of all other figures, either in the Poetical or oratory science' (xviii). The latter class includes figures like enigma, proverb, irony, hyperbole, periphrasis, and synecdoche, which is also found in the preceding class. Synecdoche asks a 'quick conceit', for 'it encombers the mind with a certain imagination what it may be that is meant, but not expressed'. But this character, in some measure, applies to all figures that involve an inversion of sense (Quintilian's 'aliud verbis, aliud sensu'), meaning 'one thing in words, another in sense'. An exception may be found in his mixt allegory, because it includes the referents of its metaphors, 'which in a full allegory

[1] See Mario Praz, *Studies in Seventeenth-Century Imagery*.

13

should not be discovered, but left at large to the readers judgment and conjecture'. For Puttenham the smaller kinds of poems are related to emotional causes and occasions.

Then poetry was not only a kind of expression but also a mode of persuasion. Puttenham (III, vii) considered it an art of persuasion. In *Of Education* Milton included poetry among the instrumental arts, logic and rhetoric, which have no proper subject matter of their own. Among his authorities, Tasso offered precedent for classifying poetry as a kind of discourse or mode of persuasion. Milton distinguished its mode from that of rhetoric only in terms of degree. Its argument 'was less subtle and fine, but more simple, sensuous, and passionate' than that of rhetoric. This distinction between rhetoric and poetry moves from persuasion towards transport as the end. Poetry is a less obscure or abstract, a more emotional, form of persuasion. Here Milton was defining poetry in its widest sense, where it seemed to be an imaginative form of rhetoric related to Bacon's allusive or parabolic conception of poetry. The fictions of poets had special efficacy, as Bacon said, 'because reason cannot be so sensible, nor examples so fit'. In expression this power required the 'figurative conveyance' of Puttenham; the 'Figurative way', as Dryden reiterated, 'is for the Passions'.

For Puttenham dissembling figures have the capacity to handle what Gascoigne calls 'some depth of devise in the Invention'. Gascoigne himself named allegory as a means to wit or 'aliquid salis'. When poetry was commonly regarded as fiction with a rhetorical end, its rhetorical forms were found in figures involving the dissimulation of tropes. Later John Hoskins finds dissimulation rather in figures that involve the use of discords or contraries, such as catachresis, irony, paradox, or litotes—all more or less fashionable. His own verse illustrates this turn of wit, whether in his well-known 'Absence', which has been attributed to Donne, or in his lesser-known epigram 'Of the Loss of Time':

If life be time that here is spent,
And time on earth be cast away,
Who so his time hath here misspent

Hath hastned his own dying day;
So it doth prove a killing crime
To massacre our living time.

If doing nought be like to death,
Of him that doth Camelion-wise
Take only pains to draw his breath,
The passers-by may pasquilize,
Not here he lives: but here he dies.

As amplification or the means to force, these figures share in part
the object of paradox, 'to stir admiration in the hearer and make
him think it a strange harmony which must be expressed in such
discords'. Like Puttenham's overlapping groups, most of them
make some demand upon the understanding, and might be classed
under the fashion of amplification called 'intimation', which suggests more than it expresses. Of course these figures involve an
element of surprise as well as ingenuity, and thus become figures
of wit in the modern sense. Wit may take the form of fanciful
exaggeration, resemblance, dissimilitude, incongruity, contradiction, or covert intimation, but its associations must always
involve the surprising or unexpected.

It was in Jonson's time that 'wit' as distinct from other intellectual virtues began to take on the special sense that Hobbes later
defined as 'fancy' or quickness of mind in seeing resemblances
between dissimilar things. Bacon said in the *Novum Organum* (Bk.
I, Aph. 55): 'The greatest and, perhaps, radical distinction between different men's dispositions for philosophy and the sciences
is this: that some are more vigorous and active in observing the
differences of things, others in observing their resemblances.' But
Puttenham had made phantasy or imagination basic to 'the inven-
tive part of the mind' (I, viii) and as widely creative as fancy in
Hobbes's 'Answer to Davenant'. In *Every Man out of his Humour*
(1600), which Jonson dedicated to the Inns of Court or the nurseries of Hoskins and Donne, new varieties of wit appealed to 'the
Judges of these Studies'. Here they could find much ado about
'Wit for Ingenuity' or the 'sharpness of your ingenuity' or a
witty rogue who 'confounds with his Similes'; and they could

appreciate the compliment, 'When I wrote this Poem I had Friendship with divers in your Societies.'

Some response from these nurseries is heard when Roger Tisdale of Gray's Inn dedicates his poem, *The Lawyers Philosophy*, to Donne in 1622: 'Flatterie be farre from me, as I wish my soule from Atheisme. Yet I must ingenuously confesse, as an ancient observant of your worth, that your yong daies were to me of much admiration, as these dayes are now of deserved reverance. To shew therfore my duties, it becomes me to meet you with humilitie, as one of the Churches Servants: and to shew my Love, I have thought fit to provide for you such a present, as for the present, I was able to give, and I know you doe love pure, and undefiled *Poesie*. . . . If I have soared into the Sunne, and singed my plumes, my fall will be easier in your armes. And I hope for the love of the Muses (who in your Youth initiated you their Son, and now in your Age have elected you a Patron) you will open the imbraces of favour, and graciously give me your acceptance, with a pardon for my daring into so high a Subject.' Here the Inns of Court return the compliment of Jonson, but to one of their own.

The relation between wit and ingenuity is also evident in the 'Elegies upon the Author' contributed to Donne's *Poems*. Eventually Dryden makes the general distinction (a 'school-distinction' he calls it) between 'Wit writing' or the 'faculty of imagination in the writer' and 'Wit written' or the 'product of imagination'. But although the faculty involved in poetic wit is the same as that in facetious wit, the feeling is not; it is not pure levity, but mingles levity and seriousness, or produces a mixed effect. And if metaphor is to be witty, it must capitalize on disparity as well as resemblance. This in turn produces its mixed effect. Thus, while poetic wit emphasized ingenuity it could blend serious and comic effects or violate other aspects of propriety without jeopardizing its claim to wit.

One of Donne's fellow wits may illustrate the lyric ingenuity of his time. In 'Absence' Hoskins makes his protestation against the strength, distance, and length of absence that separates him from his lady, and challenges absence to bring about any change in their relations.

Absence hear my protestation
  Against thy strength
  Distance and length,
Do what thou canst for alteration:
  For hearts of truest metal
  Absence doth join, and time doth settle.

Who loves a Mistress of right quality,
  His mind hath found
  Affections ground
Beyond time, place, and all mortality:
  To hearts that cannot vary
  Absence is present, time doth tarry:

My Senses want their outward motion
  Which now within
  Reason doth win,
Redoubled by her secret notion:
  Like rich men that take pleasure
  In hiding more than handling treasure.

By absence this good means I gain
  That I can catch her
  Where none can watch her,
In some close corner of my brain:
  There I embrace and kiss her,
  And so enjoy her, and so miss her.

He argues that absence only joins, time fixes, hearts of truest mettle. To love a mistress of true quality is to ground affections beyond time, place, and mortality, where absence is presence and time waits. What his senses lose by the absence of his mistress his reason gains, and the advantage is expressed in a variant (treasure) of the original metaphor (metal). Thus absence gives him the chance to catch her in mental privacy, and there both to kiss her and to feel her want. A touch of equivocation in 'miss' empha-sizes the surprising ambiguity of 'metal' in the protestation and points the wit. Initially the physical metaphor and the psychology are as disparate as in Donne's 'Valediction: forbidding mourning', but finally they are even more integrated.

If wit in the poet meant the imaging faculty, wit in the poem covered all of its products. But wit in the poem also had a narrow sense that designated some ingenuity of thought or expression, some exploitation of surprise. Wit in this sense was a product of fancy or thought, not of observation; or what Dryden called 'sharpness of conceit' as opposed to wit in the larger sense of representation. This wit operated in poetry by unexpected unions or contrasts of diverse ideas or images; it served to energize, complicate, or qualify the emotional effect. It belonged to a mode of imagination that seeks a unity of comprehension rather than of selection among the various aspects of a subject; hence its concern with the hidden relations that connect the most diverse objects or feelings. This unity of comprehension may explain Dryden's late espousal of tragi-comedy. Ultimately this wit came to be regarded as inconsistent with seriousness and hence to be restricted to the amusing. Our main subject is wit in its narrow sense, but this cannot be treated apart from the broader subject of the proper wit of poetry, which was the central expressive problem of the century. In the mock-heroic, in fact, the comic invention itself assumes the qualities of wit in the narrower sense, and the discord is found in the subject.

In the eighteenth century Bishop Hurd, in his essay *On Poetical Imitation*, developed Dryden's distinction into the direct likeness or image based on imitation and the indirect likeness or allusion based on comparison. Hurd found the latter 'ingenious exercise of the fancy' unsuitable to the simple majesty of the epic or drama. And then he added a curious example: 'And here, by the way, it may be worth observing, in honour of a great Poet of the last century, I mean Dr. Donne, that, though agreeably to the turn of his genius, and taste of his age, he was fonder, than ever poet was, of these *secret and hidden ways* in his lesser poetry; yet when he had projected his great work *On the progress of the soul* (of which we have only the beginning) his good sense brought him out into the freer *spaces* of nature and open day-light.' Others were greater culprits: 'In this, the author of *Gondibert*, and another writer of credit, a contemporary of Donne, Sir Fulk Grevil, were not so happy.' In our time this unfinished satire by Donne has been regarded as one of his worst exhibitions of wit, but Hurd seems to confuse or enlarge his genres.

In seventeenth-century poetics to pass from wit as a faculty to its product was to pass from fancy or imagination to its creations. In them certain qualities were esteemed and thus entitled to be called good wit or fancy as Hobbes noted. The nature and qualities of these creations changed both in the theory and the practice of the century; the earlier wit came to be distinguished from the later, and the term 'wit' itself underwent a dissociation of ideas. The ingenuity which was so long regarded as basic to a good wit eventually led to a separation of the serious and facetious in its product, with different criteria for each; and propriety at last subdued ingenuity.

The statement of these differences begins in Hobbes. Although he still recognizes the ingenuity of a good fancy, he stresses the judgment or propriety which separates the facetious and the serious. The product of fancy is still wit or ingenuity in ideas or images, or Dr. Johnson's 'unexpected copulation of ideas'; the product of judgment is, and remains, propriety or decorum. Puttenham had said (III, xxiii) that decorum is judged by discretion, 'which sheweth that it resteth in the discerning part of the mind, so as he who can make the best and most differences of things by reasonable and witty distinction is to be the fittest judge or sentencer of decency'. In various figures Cowley condemns the extravagance that derives from ingenuity, and Dryden later adds the impropriety of ingenious figures in serious contexts. With him genre criticism begins in earnest, chiefly on the level of diction. Hence the course of English poetry in this century cannot be understood unless we follow the various definitions and modes of wit that explain its variety.

Milton said that 'decorum is the grand masterpiece to observe', but some of the most characteristic seventeenth-century achievements are deliberate violations of decorum. Various kinds of disproportion were employed for witty effects. Whether it was the praise of some object of disfavour like 'Black Beauty' or a more serious equation of a flea-bite with a moral act, as in Donne's famous poem, its effect depended upon some violation of propriety. It is doubtful whether 'snorted we in the seven sleepers den' was more decorous then than now. Donne could also get his effect by violating the expected decorum of the Petrarchan convention, and the Restoration could achieve another effect by a new disproportion between style and content in the pastoral. Indeed, many of Donne's effects are secured by violations of accepted decorum. The paradoxical use of amplification could extend from expression by opposites in irony to diminishing by elevation in the mock-heroic. In Donne's 'compasses' the material disproportion with lovers counts as well as the constancy of their function, and they are not intended to diminish. Both surprise and new values may be brought into the realm of significance by the materials of metaphor: witness Donne and Eliot. Thus the range of expression is extended, and often by some violation of the received decorum.

When Addison analysed wit into true wit, false wit, and mixt wit, he found mixt wit not only the most difficult to define but also a major defect of seventeenth-century models. In mixt wit, says Addison, to speak of love 'both as a Passion, and as real Fire, surprizes the Reader with those seeming Resemblances or Contradictions that make up all the Wit in this kind of Writing. Mixt Wit therefore is a Composition of Punn and true Wit.' Thus if 'true Wit generally consists in the Resemblance and Congruity of Ideas', mixt Wit involves both resemblance and incongruity, or various forms of double meaning, and even ambiguities of feeling. It is this kind of wit that embraces the most subtle and original forms of seventeenth-century wit, and hence it is the kind upon which we should centre our attention when we observe examples of the practice. The examples selected in each chapter are chosen both to illustrate such forms of wit and to represent kinds of wit important at the time. The chronology of each chapter is only approximate because the title of the chapter is partially ideological.

For Dryden the mock-heroic, as defined in his 'Discourse concerning Satire', was a form of what Addison called 'mixt Wit'.

Essentially the mock-heroic is a union of opposites, but they are not reconciled as in paradox; rather they function as implicit antithesis, the greatness of the one magnifying the littleness of the other. Wit directed to ridicule is employed to diminish, by amplification in reverse. In the mock-heroic, however, it diminishes by magnifying, not by inverse amplification. But wit was also used, as by Marvell, to modify or intensify the serious by its contrary, not simply to magnify or diminish. So used, it produced a mixed tone, and reflected a mixed mood. This was a characteristic form of mixed wit in the seventeenth century, and its mixed effect is most nearly suggested today by irony. No doubt this effect led Eliot to associate Laforgue with the Metaphysical poets. But Dryden defined the mock-heroic by separating its witty and heroic elements, and Addison later established this separation of the serious and the facetious in poetic wit. The time was ripe, for Dryden had conferred upon the Sectaries his 'Doctoral Degree of Wit'.

II

JACOBEAN WIT

In the seventeenth century fancy or the power of metaphor was often regarded as the basic power of poetry. Extended metaphor was enough to carry John Hoskins through allegory to the poet's tale. Hoskins had a reputation for epigram and for polishing writers, and so his *Directions for Speech and Style* has an interest beyond that of a mere rhetoric. Written around 1600, it gives us exceptional insight into the rhetoric of wit as it was then practised. 'A metaphor or translation', says Hoskins, 'is the friendly and neighborly borrowing of one word to express a thing with more light and better note, though not so directly and properly as the natural name of the thing meant would signify.' In the eighteenth century Corbyn Morris does not distinguish wit sufficiently from this function of metaphor. But this definition serves Hoskins to distinguish catachresis, 'now grown in fashion', for it is a bolder use of metaphor: 'It is the expressing of one matter by the name of another which is incompatible with it, and sometimes clean contrary.' This may extend to the figure *ironia*, and 'is a usual figure with the fine conversants of our time, when they strain for an extraordinary phrase.' Thus Hoskins suggests the extent to which metaphor could approach the wit of contraries in this age of paradox. It may be recalled that Hoskins on figures was still good for Thomas Blount's *Academie of Eloquence* (1654) and John Smith's *Mysterie of Rhetorick Unveiled* (1657).

When Hoskins discusses amplification or the ways of giving force to expression we discover the various employments of these elements. One way is by comparison, and this involves 'things contrary, equal, or things different'. In comparison of things equal 'there are to be searched out all the several points of a consorted equality', as in Donne's compasses. Hoskins advises: 'And you shall most of all profit by inventing matter of agreement in things most unlike, as London and a tennis court: for *in both all the gain goes to the hazard.*' Antithesis or 'Comparison of contraries is the third and most flourishing way of comparison.' But there are other ways of using contraries for emphatic expression. Irony 'in dissembling sort . . . expresseth a thing by contrary'. Litotes is a way of diminishing single terms 'by denying the contrary'; but this 'sometimes in ironious sort goes for amplification.' Even then, according to Hoskins, litotes provided 'the most usual phrases in the English tongue'. There is also 'a composition of contraries', synoeciosis or forms of seeming contradiction. 'This is a fine course to stir admiration in the hearer and make them think it a strange harmony which must be expressed in such discords.' One contrary may be affirmed to be in the other either directly in oxymoron or indirectly in paradox. Besides the reconciliation of contraries, there is the opposition of them in antithesis. We may add that the Bible trained people in the paradox as a form of feeling in which seeming contraries resolved their tension.

Another way of amplification is by intimation or implication, which 'leaves the collection of greatness to our understanding, by expressing some mark of it'. This indirect expression, which intimates more than it says, may involve some of the indirect modes already mentioned, or metaphorical modes like synecdoche, metonymy, or even hyperbole, as in Jonson's epitaphs. Hoskins certainly suggests that the union or connection of contraries, whether by catachresis or paradoxical figures, and other subtle forms of indirect speech were evidences of wit in his time.

This kind of wit is better known to us as the *discordia concors* which Dr. Johnson ascribed to the Metaphysical poets in his *Life of Cowley.* It will be recalled that he described this wit as 'a combination of dissimilar, or discovery of occult resemblances in things apparently unlike', where 'the most heterogeneous ideas are yoked by violence together'. Grounds for all of these remarks are found in Hoskins, but not grounds for the conclusion about the reader: 'though he sometimes admires, is seldom pleased'. When Hoskins wrote, such elements were yoked together by fancy or ingenuity, and the surprise of their yoking did not separate admiration and pleasure in the reader.

Of course Hoskins had rules designed to govern the use of metaphor. 'The rule of a metaphor is that it be not too bold nor too far-fetched.' This rule kept it from becoming catachresis. As to propriety, the metaphor should not be too base, unless your purpose was to diminish. Such rules were emphasized by Jonson in his *Discoveries*. They were contradicted when Donne said, 'No metaphor, no comparison is too high, none too low, too trivial, to imprint' God's sense in the mind. Thus the rules of metaphor introduce a concern with the substance of metaphor. To elevate or depress anything by translating it into something higher or lower than itself requires some criteria of status, as Puttenham had made clear. In Hoskins these are implicit in the areas from which pleasing metaphor may be drawn: 'Therefore, to delight generally, take those terms from ingenious and several professions; from ingenious arts to please the learned, and from several arts to please the learned of all sorts; as from the meteors, planets, and beasts in natural philosophy, from the stars, spheres, and their motions in astronomy, from the better part of husbandry, from the politic government of cities, from navigation, from military profession, from physic; but not out of the depth of these mysteries.' To please a literate audience and to express a thing with 'better note', these are the areas from which metaphor should be drawn. Only the final proviso might have limited Donne. The general rule is this: 'But ever (unless your purpose be to disgrace) let the word be taken from a thing of equal or greater dignity.' The exception may be illustrated by Dryden's line in *Absalom and Achitophel*, where David 'Scattered his Maker's image through the land.' The too base would presumably come from the meaner arts or lower callings. These are the criteria and subjects that were prescribed for effective metaphor at the turn of the sixteenth century. Hoskins ignores mythology and the Bible, but emphasizes ingenious arts and professions, or learning.

Nor did Hoskins forget the part played by fashion. 'It is true', he said, 'that we study according to the predominancy of courtly inclinations: whilst mathematics were in request, all our similitudes came from lines, circles, and angles; whilst moral philosophy is now a while spoken of, it is rudeness not to be sententious.' Those who are rigid for decorum would do well to ponder the main concerns of Hoskins in relation to the practice of his time. His care for the sources of metaphor will remain important to those concerned with the proper wit of poetry.

From Hoskins poetic wit may be tentatively defined as the power of creating emotional surprise by the unexpected combination or contrast of generally diverse ideas or images, especially of incompatibles or contraries. It is often the exploitation of a latent resemblance between incompatibles which capitalizes on the contrast (catachresis) or a reconciliation of contraries which capitalizes on the union (paradox). Both can produce emotional surprise and express mixed feelings. In irony the wit of contraries takes on an inverted form and becomes a kind of reverse metaphor. It has the same powers as those above. In disjunctive form this wit becomes pure antithesis and loses its ambiguity. It can produce emotional surprise, but expresses sharp contrasts of feeling rather than equivocal feeling.

Coleridge's definition of wit is often cited: 'It arises in detecting the identity in dissimilar things.' But this might have defined catachresis in the seventeenth century. If the pleasure of wit is intellectual surprise, there are other ways of producing it. If this effect is essential to wit, it is put to emotional use in poetry, especially by imagery. Of course, even to speak of sardonic wit is to indicate an emotional colouring. But if metaphor is to be witty, it must capitalize on disparity as well as resemblance. However, when the disparity between the terms of a metaphor becomes real incongruity, the serious effect is threatened. The Metaphysical poets employed various forms of intellectual surprise to sharpen perception in the reader and to qualify emotion in the poet.

Hoskins used Sidney's *Arcadia* to illustrate all the figures of rhetoric. Fulke Greville in his *Life of Sidney* is rather critical of this kind of wit, because he 'conceived these delicate Images to be over-abundantly furnished in all Languages already'; and so he avoids, in his tragedies, 'the strangeness, or perplexedness of witty Fictions; In which the affections, or imagination, may perchance find exercise, and entertainment, but the memory and judgement no enriching at all.' He leaves the images of wit to Sidney, but argues that 'his Arcadian Romanties' had a moral purpose. He would be less fanciful because he writes for those who have known adversity: 'For my own part, I found my creeping Genius more fixed upon the Images of Life, than the Images of Wit, and therefore chose not to write to them on whose foot the black Oxe had not already trod, as the Proverbe is, but to those only, that are weather-beaten in the Sea of this World, such as having lost the sight of their Gardens, and groves, study to saile on a right course among Rocks, and quick-sands' (ed. Smith, p. 224). Despite his praise, Greville seems to have felt that the *Arcadia* was not serious enough, or at least in its images of wit. In 1600 Jonson satirized it as the standard of wit for Fastidius Briske. Greville resembles Bacon in his view of poetry. He prefers the kind in which imagination is not 'extremely licensed', but more tied to 'the nature of things'. His wit inclines to the sententious and the ironic.

Greville affords an interesting reflection of the poetic ambiguities of his time. He suggests in his *Life of Sidney* some of the modes of composition that were employed. His verse treatises, he tells us, were originally intended to supply choruses for his tragedies; but he confesses, 'after I had once ventured upon this spreading *Ocean* of Images, my apprehensive youth, for lack of a well touched compasse, did easily wander beyond proportion'. Hence he was obliged 'to change their places', or treat them separately. Then he becomes particular about the revision of his *Treatise of Monarchy*. The hazards which its subject presented, and which subsequently delayed its publication, now delayed its revision; but presently, out of vanity, he began to give it a richer dress: 'But while these clothes were in making, I perceived that cost would but draw more curious eyes to observe deformities. So that from these checks a new counsell rose up in me, to take away all opinion of seriousnesse from these perplexed pedegrees;

and to this end carelessly cast them into that hypocriticall figure *Ironia*, wherein men commonly (to keep above their workes) seeme to make toies of the utmost they can doe' (ed. Smith, p. 153).

Notice the motivation of this figure before we observe its effect. 'And yet againe, in that confusing mist, when I beheld this grave subject (which should draw reverence and attention) to bee over-spangled with lightnesse, I forced in examples of the Roman gravity, and greatnesse, the harsh severity of the *Lacedemonian* Governement; the riches of the *Athenian* learning, wit, and industry; and like a man that plaies divers parts upon severall hints, left all the indigested crudities, equally applied to Kings, or Tyrants: whereas in every cleere judgement, the right line had beene sufficient enough to discover the crooked; if the image of it could have proved credible to men.' Perhaps the right line would have discovered the crooked if the confusion of the irony had not been confounded by these additions. Both in motive and effect, this use of ironic levity suggests the kind of sophistication that may confront us in the poetic composition of this time. Here dissimulation and levity cloak the didactic gravity of the poet, and seem to make toys of the utmost he can do.

Samuel Butler, in his 'Miscellaneous Observations', gives a similar impression of Donne: 'Dr Don's writings are like Voluntary or Prelude in which a man is not ty'd to any particular Designe of Air; but may change his key or moode at pleasure: So his compositions seeme to have been written without any particular Scope.' This says in its way what modern critics have said in theirs about the mercurial changes in Donne. Pierre Legouis, however, would argue that after composing his first stanza freely, Donne tied himself to a 'particular Designe of Air'. Certainly Donne's literary principles resembled those of Bacon: that 'Rhetorique will make absent and remote things present to your understanding' and that 'Poetry is a counterfeit Creation, and makes things that are not, as though they were.'

Butler once used the same comparison in his *Characters*, that of 'A Drole': 'He is excellent at Voluntary and Prelude; but has no Skill in Composition. He will run Divisions upon any Ground very dextrously; but now and then mistakes a *Flat* for a *Sharp*. He has a great deal of Wit, but it is not at his own disposing, nor can he command it when he pleases, unless it be in the Humour. His Fancy is counter-changed between Jest and Earnest; and the *Earnest* lies always in the *Jest*, and the *Jest* in the *Earnest*.' Some critics might argue that this is even more apt for Donne, but it may help to explain what Butler means by the lack of 'any particular Scope'. In his view Donne seems also to have been guilty of the lack of integration about which Sidney complained in the poetry of his time. If this runs counter to the modern view of argument in Donne, it may serve to emphasize the impression which the unexpected once created in his poetry.

* 2 *

In Fulke Greville the Petrarchan is already getting lost in the philosopher. *Sententia* becomes a style in him, and the words of Hoskins may be applied: 'whilst moral philosophy is now a while spoken of, it is rudeness not to be sententious. And for my part, I'll make one. I have used and outworn six several styles since I was first Fellow of New College, and am yet able to bear the fashion of writing company. Let our age, therefore, only speak morally, and let the next age live morally.' Certainly Greville cultivates the antithetic rhetoric of sententious writing, and in his use of metaphor resembles Bacon more than Donne.

In rejecting Petrarchan 'images of wit' he rejected their illusion both in style and matter. His power resided not in fanciful allusion, but in naked words that condensed his meaning, sometimes in metaphor. After his early verse, he did not find his mistress in his Muse. Greville gives the sententia in lyrics the force which it exerts in the plays of Webster, chiefly by startling reductions of feeling to a sentence, as in *Caelica* LXXXVI: 'Life is a Top which whipping Sorrow driveth.'

But even in an early sonnet, like the famous *Caelica* XXII, he can complicate the feeling by a witty Biblical allusion:

> *Must I now lead an idle life in wishes?*
> *And follow* Cupid *for his loaves, and fishes?*

Neither to be one among five thousand nor dependent on miracles is an unambiguous prospect in love. His disillusion ends in the stanza of greatest charm, and finds expression in sententious form:

> *Was it for this that I might* Myra *see*
> *Washing the water with her beauties, white?*
> *Yet would she never write her love to me;*
> *Thinks wit of change while thoughts are in delight?*
> *Mad Girles must safely love, as they may leave,*
> *No man can print a kisse, lines may deceive.*

The impulse to cynicism and to epigram are simultaneous. The paradoxical inversion of washing has some striking parallels. Milton in *Il Penseroso* says of Sleep:

> *And let som strange mysterious dream,*
> *Wave at his Wings in Airy stream.*

Marvell in *The Garden* says of the soul:

> *Waves in its Plumes the various Light.*

The action in each case takes an unexpected form and establishes unexpected relations.

In one of his best love sonnets, *Caelica* LXIX, Greville works out a parallel between the macrocosm and the microcosm that explains and amplifies the contradictions of his love in a series of paradoxes. He begins with revolution in the heavens.

> *When all this* All *doth passe from age to age,*
> *And revolution in a circle turne,*
> *Then heavenly Justice doth appeare like rage,*
> *The Caves doe roare, the very Seas doe burne,*
> *Glory growes darke, the Sunne becomes a night,*
> *And makes this great world feele a greater might.*
>
> *When Love doth change his seat from heart to heart,*
> *And worth about the wheele of Fortune goes,*
> *Grace is diseas'd, desert seemes overthwart,*
> *Vowes are forlorne, and truth doth credit lose,*
> *Chance then gives Law, Desire must be wise,*
> *And looke more wayes than one, or lose her eyes.*

My age of joy is past, of woe begunne,
Absence my presence is, strangenesse my grace,
With them that walke against me, is my Sunne:
The wheele is turn'd, I hold the lowest place,
*   What can be good to me since my love is,*
*   To doe me harme, content to doe amisse?*

Thus he gets from the big wheel to the little wheel and a Donnian ending, but not before he has defined his state, like Donne, by opposites. The first line accumulates the power of Greville's naked word, but the revolution itself is given a dramatic metaphorical turn by the line, 'With them that walke against me, is my Sunne.' Indeed, this is the antipodal climax of the basic conceit.

One of the best religious sonnets in *Caelica* is no. LXXXVII, in which death for the lust of life is seen as the conflict between time and eternity. It centres in a passage from the 'earthly lanthorne' to the 'eternal Glasse':

When as Mans life, the light of humane lust,
In socket of his earthly lanthorne burnes,
That all this glory unto ashes must,
And generation to corruption turnes;
*   Then fond desires that onely feare their end,*
*   Doe vainely wish for life, but to amend.*

And when this life is from the body fled,
To see it selfe in that eternall Glasse,
Where time doth end, and thoughts accuse the dead,
Where all to come, is one with all that was;
*   Then living men aske how he left his breath,*
*   That while he lived never thought of death.*

Here Greville anticipates Eliot in saying that life is redeemable only in time, for time past and time future collapse into eternity. Again Greville's power is greatest in his sententious statement. His 'Images of Life' take form in a moral rhetoric pointed by the abstract word, sustained by the vivid metaphor.

Greville could never make peace, like Bacon, between the rival claims of heaven and earth. This conflict was the source of his

bitterness and his wisdom. It was most sharply expressed in the
'Chorus Sacerdotum' of *Mustapha* (1633).

> *Oh wearisome Condition of Humanity!*
> *Borne under one Law, to another bound:*
> *Vainely begot, and yet forbidden vanity;*
> *Created sicke, commanded to be sound:*
> *What meaneth Nature by these diverse Lawes?*
> *Passion and Reason, selfe-division cause:*
> *Is it the marke or Majesty of Power*
> *To make offences that it may forgive?*
> *Nature herselfe doth her owne selfe defloure,*
> *To hate those errours she her selfe doth give.*
> *For how should man thinke that, he may not doe*
> *If Nature did not faile, and punish too?*
> *Tyrant to others, to her selfe unjust,*
> *Onely commands things difficult and hard;*
> *Forbids us all things which it knowes is lust,*
> *Makes easie paines, unpossible reward.*
> *If Nature did not take delight in blood,*
> *She would have made more easie wayes to good.*
> *We that are bound by vowes, and by Promotion,*
> *With pompe of holy Sacrifice and rites,*
> *To teach beliefe in good and still devotion,*
> *To preach of Heaven's wonders, and delights:*
> *Yet when each of us in his own heart lookes,*
> *He findes the God there, farre unlike his Bookes.*

Here the wit of contradiction is founded in the nature of things
and thus becomes unusually poignant. This chorus echoed
through the century, but ironically it came to sound atheistic as
well as natural to Restoration ears. It joined Browne's *Religio
Medici* as a libertine text, for example, in the sermons of Tillotson.[1]

In temper Greville seems closer to Donne than to Sidney, but

[1] See *Works* (London, 1820), Vol. II, Ser. 28, and Vol. VIII, Ser. 193; or
Guy Holland (John Sergeant), *The Grand Prerogative of Human Nature*,
London, 1653.

in wit he is both less simple than Sidney and less complex than Donne. In Donne the surprise of wit may be either sudden as in point, or delayed as in poetic epigram, or pervasive as in irony. His argument is commonly employed as a mode of surprise rather than of persuasion, as in his prose paradoxes; its end is to point or magnify his emotions rather than to prove them. He uses logic as a means of developing or exploiting the paradoxes of thought and feeling; of thought in the *Paradoxes and Problems*, of feeling in the *Songs and Sonnets*. Even in a subtle argument like that of 'The Extasie' there is a surprising reversal of direction and means in the discovery of love—from seen to unseen to seen. The rhetoric of his emotions constantly takes unexpected forms and develops unexpected but not incoherent consequences. Dissimilar ideas suddenly associated can produce both wit and insight or convey the ironies of feeling. These are functions of the so-called conceit in Donne. In force of style, said Hoskins the wit, 'you shall most of all profit by inventing matter of agreement in things most unlike'.

Although Donne spoke lightly of evaporating his wit and more seriously of venting his wit, it was for him a way of resolving tensions as well as paradoxes, and included the argumentative element in his poetry. These arguments are no less subjective or witty than any other element in his poetry, but they can explore and define more variable, complicated, or conflicting emotions. The delayed surprise of his arguments builds upon suspense, which gives them a dramatic quality. Their development is often punctuated by the sudden surprise which discovers novel perceptions, but their main purpose is to amplify both the subtlety and the energy of his emotions. This may be seen in 'Lovers Infiniteness', where it is the mutable character of lovers rather than of love that requires logical exploration before the relative nature of 'all' can be established for them and their duality conquered.

In reading Donne's poems we should remember that his prose paradoxes run a gamut from those that 'carry with them a confession of their lightness' to the serious *Biathanatos*. A poem like 'The Indifferent' belongs at the lighter end of this gamut, and is in fact related to 'A Defence of Womens Inconstancy'. The speaker develops his indifference to a whole series of opposites that might be expected to limit love, but discovers only one opposite to which he is not indifferent, and that is constancy. This new heresy in love, which Venus had not heard before, is to be punished by making its few victims true to a false love. The loss involved in this heresy, 'Love's sweetest part, Variety', is developed at length in the prose paradox, which is more argumentative. But had this play of wit any serious intent? Donne once explained that his paradoxes 'are rather alarums to truth to arme her than enemies'; they are meant to test, to challenge, or to discover weakness, certainly to be provocative. Thus 'The Indifferent' is breaking the stereotype of Petrarchan love, and indeed suggesting, for all its wit, that no stereotype can limit or confine love.

A more serious use of definition by opposites is found in 'Negative Love'. This poem is singular in Donne's work because his most comprehensive pair of opposites, body and soul, for once fail to define love; their faculties prove inadequate.

> *I never stoop'd so low, as they*
> *Which on an eye, cheek, lip, can prey,*
>   *Seldom to them, which soar no higher*
>   *Than virtue or the mind to admire,*
> *For sense, and understanding may*
>   *Know, what gives fuel to their fire:*
> *My love, though silly, is more brave,*
> *For may I miss, whene'er I crave,*
> *If I know yet what I would have.*

He knew by sense in 'Love's Growth' and by understanding in 'The Undertaking'; he contrasted the two ways in 'A Valediction: forbidding mourning.' Now neither object, neither faculty, can define his love; it must be defined another way.

> *If that be simply perfectest*
> *Which can by no way be exprest*
>   *But* Negatives, *my love is so.*
>   *To All, which all love, I say no.*

If any who decipher best.
What we know not, ourselves, can know,
Let him teach me that nothing; this
As yet my ease, and comfort is,
Though I speed not, I cannot miss.

Perfection which must be expressed by negatives naturally escapes definition or knowledge, and so he challenges those who profess self-knowledge to teach him the unknowable. Yet he has some consolation: though he cannot speed in understanding, he cannot miss in practice; he acts by instinct. Thus by negating his usual mode of analysis he increases the ultimate mystery of love as he scorns even the triumph of 'A Valediction: forbidding mourning'.

In 'Air and Angels' body and soul are used to define love positively, in conjunction with the idea that air provides body for angels. The first stanza moves from soul to body in describing his love, or from 'some lovely glorious nothing' to an embodiment in her physical charms. The second stanza discovers the disability of both extremes: neither in pure soul nor in pure body can love inhere or be fixed. His dilemma is stated with wonderful precision:

For, nor in nothing, nor in things
Extreme, and scatt'ring bright, can love inhere.

Only her love can be his love's sphere, and only by assuming the angelic body or sphere which manifests an angel to man. Between an angel and man air is a necessary corporeal medium; such a medium is required likewise in the love of man and woman, and it does not defile woman. For 'some depth of devise in the Invention' this poem would have pleased Gascoigne as much as it has baffled readers, since it begins in Platonism and ends in compromise.

'A Valediction: forbidding mourning' relates parting to body and soul, first as in the parting of death. To be demonstrative would profane their love. The movement beginning in death leads into the movements of heaven and earth, and these serve to define earthly and heavenly lovers. Sublunary love depends wholly upon body, and so cannot endure separation; but love of the soul can, because it conquers the physical disabilities. Both similes admit the physical element—which is crucial to the other love—and conquer it. First on the basis of their unity as lovers:

> *Our two souls therefore, which are one,*
> *Though I must go, endure not yet*
> *A breach, but an expansion,*
> *Like gold to aery thinness beat.*

Then on the basis of their duality as persons:

> *If they be two, they are two so*
> *As stiff twin compasses are two,*
> *Thy soul the fixed foot, makes no show*
> *To move, but doth, if th' other do.*

There is no real separation in either case. The compass figure reduces to concrete form the earlier claim, 'Inter-assurèd of the mind.' Thus the movement of parting, like death, extends to heaven and earth, and is defined by body and soul.

'Holy Sonnet XIX' returns to a tissue of paradoxes like 'The Indifferent', culminating in an analogy with ague, which reaches a climax in Christian fear and paradox: 'Those are my best days, when I shake with fear.' And the point turns upon an ambiguity. This illustration of the use of opposites shows that Donne achieves the surprise of wit by various kinds of unexpected development. Besides surprising paradox, he may employ ingenious similitudes, ambiguity of word or thing, basic analogy, deceptive argument, turns on a latent mood, or combinations of such means. In 'Women's Constancy', for example, the attitude which produces the surprise ending is implicit in the exaggerated first line, 'Now thou hast lov'd me one whole day.'

Surprising paradox is a common mode of wit in Donne. In 'The Undertaking' the brave thing he has done is daring to love virtue in woman, and the braver deed that ensues is to conceal this love of virtue. In 'The Sun Rising' the sun, ruler of time and space, is only the subject of lovers, and may benefit by changing his world

for theirs. Incidentally, this poem illustrates the fallacy of confusing lyric poetry and history on the part of annotators who try
to date such poems by pseudo-allusions.

A finer poem with a similar basis is 'The Anniversary', which
explores the relation of love to time. Their love is superior to
time, but not their bodies. In the first stanza the law of the sublunary world, dissolution, finds an exception: 'Only our love hath
no decay.' But the second stanza does not exempt their bodies
from this law. Their souls, however, will prove their love after
death. Yet in heaven where all are blessed, they will not be
unique, as in the world of time. Hence time is the true measure
of their triumph. The argument thus leads to a surprising reversal,
which establishes the proper significance of 'anniversary'. Paradox gets another turn in 'Holy Sonnet III', where the speaker
would recover the sighs and tears he spent in his amorous idolatry in order to spend them more fruitfully in his religious peni-
tence. Other sinners get some relief because the 'effect and cause,
the punishment and sin' are not the same for them.

In the analogical mode of wit 'Love's Alchemy' works out the
analogy between the two terms of the title, but in 'Twickenham
Garden' a lady's relation to him is disclosed in the metaphor of
her garden's effect upon him. In 'A Fever' death is defined relative to the world, and then the implications of a fever in the
beloved are unfolded by resemblances between her and the world.
Lastly, the fever is found to be like the speaker in preferring her
to the world, though it be only for a short time:

> *For I had rather owner be*
> *Of thee one hour, than all else ever.*

'The Canonization' expands its concept as it might apply to love.
Canonization necessitates the rejection of worldly values, explains
the opposition between the worldly and unworldly, and becomes
the idealizing metaphor of the poem.

More complicated is 'A Nocturnal upon St. Lucy's Day', which
points to a midnight service for the holiday of this minor saint of
love. The effect of his Lucy's death on the speaker is elaborated in
the metaphor of this time in nature and religion, and is directed

by the idea of privation. The passing of all principles of being for him reduces him to a descent in the scale of being, and so for the death of nature he becomes the inscription which gives the tomb meaning. Lovers to be should study him, 'In whom love wrought new alchemy'. In this antithesis to 'Love's Alchemy' he exists only in terms of the privation of presence, light, life. All others derive their being, or 'life, soul, form, spirit', from all things; only he is, by love's limbec, the grave of all that is nothing. Often their tears drowned their world, their neglect of each other withdrew their formal principle, or their absences left their bodies without souls. By her death he has become the quintessence of the first nothing. He has none of the properties that might establish him as man, beast, plant, or stone; even an ordinary nothing, like shadow, requires light and a body to produce it. Yet he is none, and his sun will not renew. But lovers for whom the lesser sun has run to Capricorn

> *To fetch new lust, and give it you,*
> *Enjoy your summer all.*

His Lucy enjoys her long night, and he must prepare towards the darkness of her festival. In this poem virtuosity sounds the depths.

Other varieties of this ingenious mode are easily found. In 'The Damp' the title is related to love as the destructive effect of her picture, but she has a better way to kill, and so the relation is explored by the ambiguity of 'kill'. In 'The Dissolution' the lovers' relation is expanded by the doctrine of the four elements. In 'The Good-Morrow' love is like waking to a new day, a new life, a new world; it is a growing discovery. 'The Cross', which is addressed to the Puritans, makes the cross as difficult to escape as Browne makes the quincunx in *The Garden of Cyrus*. For both it is an exercise in emblematic wit that reaches metaphysical implications. 'The Funeral' is directed by the possible meanings of a wreath of hair as the sign of a lover's fate, whether that of subject, prisoner, or martyr—all forms of constraint.

The last relationship is extended in 'The Relique', which names the basic analogy. Love relics, like religious relics, have their miracles; and these are the miracles associated with 'a bracelet of

bright hair about the bone.' It is an extraordinary poem, the
apotheosis of his macabre imagination.

> When my grave is broke up again
> Some second guest to entertain,
> (For graves have learn'd that woman-head
> To be to more than one a Bed)
> And he that digs it, spies
> A bracelet of bright hair about the bone,
> Will he not let us alone,
> And think that there a loving couple lies,
> Who thought that this device might be some way
> To make their souls, at the last busy day,
> Meet at this grave, and make a little stay?
>
> If this fall in a time, or land,
> Where mis-devotion doth command,
> Then, he that digs us up, will bring
> Us, to the Bishop, and the King,
> To make us Reliques; then
> Thou shalt be a Mary Magdalen, and I
> A something else thereby;
> All women shall adore us, and some men;
> And since at such time, miracles are sought,
> I would have that age by this paper taught
> What miracles we harmless lovers wrought.
>
> First, we lov'd well and faithfully,
> Yet knew not what we lov'd, nor why,
> Difference of sex no more we knew,
> Than our Guardian Angels do;
> Coming and going, we
> Perchance might kiss, but not between those meals;
> Our hands ne'er touched the seals,
> Which nature, injur'd by late law, sets free:
> These miracles we did; but now alas,
> All measure, and all language, I should pass,
> Should I tell what a miracle she was.

Indeed this is Donne in epitome, running the whole gamut of his wit. Knowing only the ceremonial kiss, he masks the ambiguity of his relationship in the line, 'A something else thereby', and then reveals it in the miracles they did.

A deceptive mode of argument is found in 'The Prohibition'. The extremes of love and hate are both shown to be destructive; hence they must be combined to negate their consequences. 'Air and Angels', although highly metaphorical, also develops extremes which have to be mediated. 'Lovers' Infiniteness' exhausts logically the limitations of regarding love as an exchange. The finite has parts, but not the infinite; hence the desires of lovers cannot be satisfied by exchange, which depends upon parts. Only by union can they transcend the finite limitations of duality in love, for 'all' will no longer be relative or divisible when they are 'one, and one another's All'. A more teasing or less explicit logic underlies 'A Valediction: forbidding mourning'. What is forbidden affects the manner of parting, which involves movement, which involves fear, which relates to the separation of body and soul: body cannot endure absence in love, but soul can. If our souls are one, they are superior to separation; if they are two, they may still be united in response. Hence there is no need for mourning.

Supreme exhibits in their respective modes are found in two religious poems. In the 'Hymn to God my God, in my Sickness' the basic figure is a passage or journey from west to east, from death to resurrection or the Holy room. This figure connects door, discovery, fever, straits, West, East, Paradise, Calvary, the first Adam with the last. As Donne preached in the Holy room on earth, so he now prepares himself for the next world by accepting the necessity of pain and death, or in his Text, 'Therefore that He may raise the Lord throws down.' Thus by means of the wit of resemblance he comes to understand the last great paradox.

'Good Friday, 1613, Riding Westward' is another variant on the paradox that going westward ultimately means going eastward. Here a conflict between the world and devotion is worked out in terms of motions, first of the spheres, and then of conflicting motives. The westward motion is finally excused as a preparation for the eastward. In terms of the opening figure his original movement becomes proper, not foreign. Here again the paradoxical surprise is developed by the wit of resemblance playing upon the basic antithesis.

An example of the wit of discordant feeling is found in 'Holy Sonnet XVII', in which feeling for his wife becomes the attraction towards God. The contrariety of his feelings is disclosed by means of discordant objects or claims of feeling. Now the death of his good has set his mind wholly on heaven, whence she has been early ravished.

> *Here the admiring her my mind did whet*
> *To seek Thee God; so streams do show their head;*
> *But though I have found Thee, and Thou my thirst hast fed,*
> *A holy thirsty dropsy melts me yet.*

For his love is not satisfied, though he feels that God woos his soul both for his beloved and against potential rivals.

> *But why should I beg more Love, when as Thou*
> *Dost woo my soul for hers; off'ring all Thine:*
> *And dost not only fear lest I allow*
> *My Love to Saints and Angels, things divine,*
> *But in Thy tender jealousy dost doubt*
> *Lest the World, Flesh, yea Devil put Thee out.*

In the love of God it is one thing to be jealous of Catholic 'Saints and Angels, things divine,' but quite another to fear even the rivals of his third *Satire*. Thus he gives an oblique development to the ambiguities of feeling involved in saying 'my good is dead'. Just such discords often lend sharpness to his feelings as well as point to their reconciliation.

Donne's ingenuity can create out of a fever different conceits for some of his most moving poems. In 'A Fever' he takes this simple definition, 'To leave this world behind, is death', and works out the significance of her fever to the world by means of the possible implications of this relationship. The hyperbole of *An Anatomy of the World* is already here. In the 'Hymn to God my

God, in my Sickness' fever again—'*Per fretum febris*, by these straits to die'—opens out into macrocosmic imagery, but this time it leads to that 'Holy room', not to passing possession of the beloved. To these examples we may add the ague of 'Holy Sonnet XIX'.

The simple idea of an exchange can run through a wide gamut of mood and wit in Donne. In 'Love's Usury' a cynical bargain is made with the God of Love to let his lust reign until his grey hairs are equal with his brown, and then he will give twenty to one odds as a victim of the shame and pain of love. Spare him any emotional involvement now, and he will even accept one that loves him. In 'Lovers' Infiniteness' the exchange of love proves frustrating because of the unlimited nature of lovers. Another solution of the problems created by their duality has to be sought:

> *But we will have a way more liberal,*
> *Than changing hearts, to join them, so we shall*
> *Be one, and one another's All.*

'Love's Exchange' gives another turn to the idea of bargaining with love. First, Love is scolded for being niggardly; all other devils give at least the art of the vice for which souls sell themselves. But he asks no favours, only Love's blindness, 'in eyes and mind', so that he may not know his shame. If Love gives nothing, he cannot complain because he gave Love so much trouble, 'Having put Love at last to show this face', and outdo Marlowe:

> *This face, by which he could command*
> *And change th' idolatry of any land,*
> *This face, which whereso'er it comes,*
> *Can call vow'd men from cloisters, dead from tombs,*
> *And melt both Poles at once, and store*
> *Deserts with cities, and make more*
> *Mines in the earth, than Quarries were before.*

Hence Love is furious and would make an example of him, but Love has taken the wrong way:

JACOBEAN WIT

If th' unborn
Must learn, by my being cut up, and torn:
Kill, and dissect me, Love; for this
Torture against thine own end is,
Rack'd carcasses make ill Anatomies.

The feelings rather than the turns of argument are more complicated in this poem than in 'Lovers' Infiniteness', and the wit is
therefore more incisive.

Donne can put the same bit of learning to a variety of ingenious
uses. For example, his use of 'mixtures' depends upon the idea
that not only what is simple, such as the soul, cannot be dissolved,
but also compounds between whose elements there is no contrariety, such as heavenly bodies; other mixtures are subject to the
sublunary world of change and decay. The conclusion of 'The
Good-Morrow' makes use of this doctrine to prevent any dissolution in love. In 'Love's Growth' the first stanza involves this
doctrine to prove that love is not pure, but a mixture:

Love's not so pure, and abstract, as they use
To say, which have no Mistress but their Muse.

Yet the second stanza still keeps the doctrine in view when it
concludes that love is more like the heavens than the sublunary
grass. More paradoxical is the use made of this doctrine in 'The
Dream'. This antithesis to 'Air and Angels' is paradoxical enough
in excusing him for mistaking his lady for an angel:

I must confess, it could not choose but be
Profane, to think thee anything but thee.

But that paradox is capped when he doubts his carnal Angel:

That love is weak, where fear's as strong as he;
'Tis not all spirit, pure, and brave,
If mixture it of Fear, Shame, Honour, *have.*

Paradox enters into the very elements of this mixture, and indeed
of its pseudo-Platonism. In fact, part of Donne's wit is to give
the illusion of using Petrarchan conventions even as he mocks
them. This is the *coup de grâce* of his anti-Petrarchism.

III

CAROLINE WIT

* I *

By Caroline times Donne's revolt against the conventions of the Elizabethan sonneteers began to be described as a rejection of classical imitation and hence to oppose his verse to the developments of Ben Jonson. Carew's elegy on Donne is the best statement of his reputation at this time. There Donne is celebrated because he rejected the current pedantry of the Muses: disdained the inspiration both of Anacreon and of Pindar; scorned classical thefts and puns; wrote neither the little ode nor the great ode, and refused to draw upon the storehouse of classical myth, which gave poets a ready means of treating their subjects. Rather he is praised for his originality, for his 'rich and pregnant phansie', and his 'masculine expression', which the ancients would have imitated if they had known them. Instead, 'Our superstitious fooles admire and hold / Their lead more precious, then thy burnish't Gold.' For Carew, as for Sprat later, their myths are 'well-nigh consumed', their Nature almost worn out. Donne substituted, but Jonson avoided, what Sprat called 'the Sciences of mens Brains'. By now Donne is clearly aligned against classical imitation and therefore at odds with the tribe of Ben.

Drummond of Hawthornden may speak for the opposition. In a letter to Dr. Arthur Johnston he spoke of poetry at about the same time as Carew: 'In vain have some Men of late (Transformers of every Thing) consulted upon her Reformation, and endeavoured to abstract her to Metaphysical Idea's, and Scholastical Quiddities, denuding her of her own Habits, and those Ornaments with which she hath amused the World some Thousand Years. Poesy is not a Thing that is yet in the finding and search,

or which may be otherwise found out, being already conde-
scended upon by all Nations, and as it were established *jure
Gentium*, amongst Greeks, Romans, Italians, French, Spaniards.
Neither do I think that a good Piece of Poesy, which Homer,
Virgil, Ovid, Petrarch, Bartas, Ronsard, Boscan, Garcilasso (if
they were alive, and had that Language) could not understand,
and reach the Sense of the Writer. . . . What is not like the
Ancients and conform to those Rules which hath been agreed
unto by all Times, may (indeed) be something like unto Poesy, but
it is no more Poesy than a Monster is a Man. Monsters breed
Admiration at the First. . . . For the like Cause it may be thought
these Men found out their new Poesy differing from the Matters,
Manners, and Rules of former Ages. . . . The Verses of Camillus
Quernus as they are imitated by Strada seem very plausible and
to Admiration to some, but how far they are off right Poesy
Children may guess. These Men's new Conceptions approach
nearer his, than to the Majesty and Stateliness of the great Poets.'
If these men were not Marinists, who were anti-Petrarchists, they
were probably the unnamed English. Drummond names Petrarch in the European tradition, but not Marino, despite his own
translations. Later Camillo Querno appears in Pope's *Dunciad*
(II) as a parallel to Colley Cibber:

> *Not with more glee, by hands Pontific crown'd*
> *With scarlet hats wide-waving circled round,*
> *Rome in her Capitol saw Querno sit,*
> *Thron'd on sev'n hills, the Antichrist of wit.*

It is not clear that Drummond included Donne among the anti-
Petrarchists, but he did not include him among the imitators, the
best of whom he thought Sidney, Alexander, and Daniel. In his
Conversations he speaks of Donne as follows: 'Donne among the
Anacreontick Lyricks, is Second to none, and far from all Second;
But as Anacreon doth not approach Callimachus, tho' he excels
in his own kind, nor Horace to Virgil; no more can I be brought
to think him to excel either Alexander's or Sidney's Verses: They
can hardly be compared together, treding diverse Paths; the one
flying swift, but low; the other, like the Eagle, surpassing the

Clouds. I think, if he would, he might easily be the best Epigrammatist we have found in English; of which I have not yet seen any come near the Ancients.' This appraisal puts Donne in the tradition of Anacreon and the little ode, Sidney in that of the great ode, although Carew put Donne in neither. Obviously Sidney is closer to 'right Poesy' than Donne. Drummond seems to feel that Donne is better described as an epigrammatist, though his views must have annoyed Jonson. Clearly Drummond is the voice of tradition and Carew is not. The old and the new are sharply opposed in their attitude towards the traditional habits and ornaments of poetry found in classical myth and now threatened by new veins of fancy.

Jonson is more instructive on the forms that ingenuity took. In his 'Execration upon Vulcan', for destroying his library, he enumerates the false wit that would have given Vulcan a proper motive:

> *Had I compiled from Amadis de Gaul,*
> *The Esplandians, Arthurs, Palmerins, and all*
> *The learned library of Don Quixote,*
> *And so some goodlier monster had begot;*
> *Or spun out riddles, or weaved fifty tomes*
> *Of logogriphs, and curious palindromes,*
> *Or pumped for those hard trifles, anagrams,*
> *Or eteostics, or those finer flams*
> *Of eggs, and halberds, cradles, and a hearse,*
> *A pair of scissors, and a comb in verse;*
> *Acrostics, and telestichs on jump names,*
> *Thou then hadst had some colour for thy flames,*
> *On such my serious follies. But, thou'lt say,*
> *There were some pieces of as base allay,*
> *And as false stamp there; parcels of a play. . . .*

Some of these forms Jonson could find in his copy of Puttenham's *Arte of English Poesie*, in the chapter 'Of Proportion in figure', although Puttenham called them 'courtly trifles'. Indeed, Jonson's poems reveal his own adventures into 'acrostic land', and George Herbert's poems are fertile in these forms of wit or ingenuity; but they have little, if any, place in Donne. Yet Jonson, like Donne, is more given to epigrammatic wit, although he impressed Drummond less favourably than Donne in this respect.

But even this kind of wit provoked Donne's ingenuity. In his second Elegy, 'The Anagram', a paradoxical eulogy of ugliness, he turns 'anagram' to account as a conceit for misplaced features in an ugly woman. And of this piece Drummond remarked: 'Compare Song, *Marry and Love*, &c., with Tasso's *Stanzas against Beauty*; one shall hardly know who hath the best.' Evidently some kinds of wit were not beyond Drummond's appreciation: he wrote upon the Impresa and the Anagram.

In *Timber* Jonson comments on the charge that 'some men are not witty, because they are not everywhere witty', that nothing is more foolish, and then adds: 'But now nothing is good that is natural; right and natural language seems to have least of the wit in it; that which is writhed and tortured is counted the more exquisite . . . no beauty to be had but in wresting and writhing our own tongue! Nothing is fashionable till it be deformed; and this is to write like a gentleman.' This reminds us of one of Coleridge's best-known remarks about Donne, and we could add other remarks that anticipate Addison's requirements for wit, but the chief point is that it generalizes the principle of ingenuity which Jonson satirizes in the 'Execration'. The principle and some of the examples are met again in Dryden's *Mac Flecknoe*.

Although Herbert is given to these verbal forms of wit, he asserts other aims both in his 'Jordan' poems and in his *Priest to the Temple*. Possibly the discrepancy is explained as the 'bait of pleasure' by which 'A verse may find him, who a sermon flies.' None the less their aims were similar for Herbert, and he tells us that the Country Parson by stories and sayings 'procures attention; but the character of his sermon is holiness; he is not witty, or learned, or eloquent, but holy'. His skill in catechizing involves the 'familiar illustration': 'This is the skill, and doubtless the Holy Scripture intends thus much, when it condescends to the naming of a plough, a hatchet, a bushel, leaven, boys piping and dancing; shewing that things of ordinary use are not only to serve in the way of drudgery, but to be washed, and cleansed, and serve for lights even of heavenly truths.' This suggests a different source and kind of wit from those specified by Hoskins; it is both indecorous, except in Scripture, and intentionally opposed to the learned kind in Herbert's poetry. Even 'The British Church' goes from hair 'about her eares' to a pun on 'grace'. Donne, in his *Devotions* (XIX), found in Scripture not only 'reverent simplicity' but also 'majesty of the word' involving 'peregrinations to fetch remote and precious metaphors'.

Quarles the emblem poet apologizes for his verse in *Argalus and Parthenia* (1629) because he has not affected a current form of wit that Jonson mentions in the *Execration* as 'the strong lines, that so the time doe catch', and that is later ascribed to Donne: 'In this Discourse, I have not affected to set thy understanding on the Rack, by the tyranny of *strong lines*, which (as they fabulously report of *China* dishes) are made for the third *Generation* to make use of, and are the meere itch of wit; under the colour of which, many have ventured (trusting to the Oedipean conceit of their ingenious Reader) to write *non-sense*, and feloniously father the created expositions of other men; not unlike some painters, who first made the picture, then, from the opinion of better judgments, conclude, whom it resembles.' Quarles concludes, 'These lines are strong enough for my purpose,' and so avoided the risk that Jonson prophesied—'That Donne himself, for not being understood, would perish.' But Henry Reynolds, who argued for esoteric interpretation in his *Mythomystes*, condemned the poetry of this time as 'slight flashes of ungrounded fancy'.

Reynolds was even more contemptuous of the accidents of poetry; 'such as are, what sort of Poeme may admit the blanke verse, what requires exacte rime; where the strong line (as they call it), where the gentle sortes best'. But these were not idle questions for Ben Jonson. Indeed, although he appreciated Donne's wit, he was moved to say, 'That Donne, for not keeping of accent, deserved hanging.' In the eighteenth century Thomas Gray said that Donne in his *Satires* 'observes no regularity in the pause, or in the feet of his verse, only the number of syllables is equal throughout. I suppose he thought this rough uncouth measure suited the plain familiar style of satirical poetry.' But Gray spoke after Dryden.

Donne is praised in the 'Elegies upon the Author' (1633–5) as much for wit or fancy as Jonson is later for judgment. This note is struck by Carew and maintained by others. Donne's invention is stressed no less than Jonson's tradition, and his virtues are made almost the opposite of Jonson's. It is true that Carew speaks of verse 'refined' by Donne, but this is opposed to 'ballad rime' and the 'exiled traine' of mythology, or else relates to the inventions of Donne. Once, however, the praise of Donne and Jonson finds a surprising agreement. Jasper Mayne urges the 'Poore Suburbe wits' to imitate Donne:

> *From this Muse learne to Court, whose power could move*
> *A Cloystred coldnesse, or a Vestall love,*
> *And would convey such errands to their eare,*
> *That Ladies knew no oddes to grant and heare.*

Later this Muse was condemned by Dryden for lacking such power, but Dryden never thought of offering Jonson as a substitute. Yet Richard West, brother-in-law of Thomas Randolph, says of Jonson:

> *The cringing Monsieur shall thy language vent,*
> *When he would melt his wench with compliment.*
> *Using thy phrases he may have his wish*
> *Of a coy nun, without an angry pish!*

Certainly the language of gallantry was a Caroline achievement, but it is a very uncommon theme among the eulogists of Jonson. Closer to Jonson's heart are these words in *Timber*: 'What a deal of cold business doth a man mis-spend the better part of life in! in scattering compliments, tendering visits, gathering and venting news, following feasts and plays, making a little winter-love in a dark corner.'

Yet Jonson created a vein of complimentary verse which made others his 'language vent'. A fine example, both of his verse and his complimentary wit, is found in the epigram 'To Mary Lady Wroth'. This is the very epitome of mythological wit.

Madame, had all antiquitie been lost,
* All history seal'd up, and fables crost;*
That wee had left us, nor by time, nor place,
* Least mention of a* Nymph, *a* Muse, *a* Grace,
But even their names were to bee made anew,
* Who could not but create them all, from you?*

And this he proceeds to do by way of celebrating her charms, only
to end by making her the index of all lost treasure:

So are you Nature's Index, *and restore*
I' your selfe, all treasure lost of th'age before.

Jonson cultivated the unemphatic tone, and even in hyperbole
tried to suggest the politeness of understatement. In contrast
Carew's song, 'Ask me no more', employs the Metaphysical mode
of wit within the song convention that Jonson passed on to the
Caroline poets. In this song the lady's charms become the final
causes of nature's beauties:

For in your beauties orient deep,
These Flowers as in their causes sleep.

Beneath the lyric beauty of this poem lies the equation: as effects
are to causes so nature is to you. Thus the lyric amelioration of
Jonson could soften the asperity of Donne in a Caroline poet.

And Jonson had contrived his own kind of amorous verse. He
managed to combine the opposites of the man and his genius in
the wit of 'My Picture left in Scotland'.

I doubt that Love is rather deaf than blind,
* For else it could not be,*
*   That she,*
Whom I adore so much, should so slight me,
* And cast my suit behind:*
I'm sure my language to her is as sweet,
* And all my closes meet,*
* In numbers of as subtle feet,*
* As hath the youngest he*
That sits in shadow of Apollo's tree.

Oh! but my conscious fears,
That fly my thoughts between,
Tell me that she hath seen
My hundreds of gray hairs,
Told seven and forty years,
Read so much waste, as she cannot embrace
My mountain belly, and my rocky face,
And all these, through her eyes, have stopt her ears.

This poem exploits an antithesis between his poetry and his person by means of a paradox—a reversal of mythology—on Cupid's weakness. Both the charm and the crudeness of Jonson are here, and together they underwrite the glory of the poet. Thus Jonson fashioned a witty manner of apologizing for not treating love seriously, which was not Donne's way.

The main themes of eulogy employed by the elegists of Donne are found in Carew's elegy, but some of these were anticipated by those who appeared with *Deaths Duell* in 1632. Henry King runs the changes on themes like 'Rich soule of wit, and language', the present 'Widow'd invention' or 'bankrupt Mine' of wit, the 'awfull fire' that is above 'a low pitch't phansie', and 'thy High Victorious Numbers'. Edward Hyde or Clarendon also centres upon his wit or fancy:

The Epitaphs *thou writst, have so bereft*
Our tongue of wit, there is not phansie left
Enough to weepe thee.

Indeed, Clarendon strikes the keynote for both Donne and Jonson. Despite Carew's elegy, we should not forget that for Donne's elegists Chudleigh opens on the right note:

Long since this taske of teares from you was due,
Long since, ô Poëts, he did die to you,
Or left you dead, when wit and he tooke flight
On divine wings, and soard out of your sight.

The poet was then a less compelling presence than the priest.

Jonson's reputation at his death is expressed clearly enough in the *Jonsonus Virbius* (1638). It is the same as that set down later by Clarendon in his *Life*: 'Ben Jonson's name can never be forgotten, having by his very good learning, and the severity of his nature and manners, very much reformed the stage; and indeed the English poetry itself. His natural advantages were, judgment to order and govern fancy, rather than excess of fancy, his productions being slow and upon deliberation, yet then abounding with great wit and fancy, and will live accordingly; and surely as he did exceedingly exalt the English language in eloquence, propriety, and masculine expressions, so he was the best judge of, and fittest to prescribe rules to poetry and poets, of any man, who had lived with, or before him, or since: if Mr. Cowley had not made a flight beyond all men, with that modesty yet, to ascribe much of this to the example and learning of Ben Jonson.' The same reputation, except the proviso about Cowley, is expressed in Dryden's *Essay of Dramatic Poesy*, even to the understatement of his fancy.

In the *Jonsonus Virbius*, notably in the elegies by John Beaumont and Henry King, one of the chief themes is Jonson's refinement of the language and poetry. Above all, he taught his contemporaries *simplex munditiis*, how to be neat. Another constant theme is his 'learned muse' or 'The voice most echoed by consenting men.' Great stress is likewise laid upon his judgment: 'Thy star was judgment only, and right sense,' says Cartwright. And Cartwright joins John Ford among others in praising Jonson for giving English form to our classical heritage. As Ford puts it,

> *The muses, first in Greece begot, in Rome*
> *Brought forth, our best of poets hath called home,*
> *Nurst, taught, and planted here; that Thames now sings*
> *The Delphian altars, and the sacred springs.*

The consequence for our English, says Henry King, is

> *That, thus refined and robed, it shall not spare*
> *With the full Greek or Latin to compare.*

Jonson's contemporaries compared him rather than Shakespeare

with 'all, that insolent Greece, or haughty Rome / Sent forth, or
since did from their ashes come.' Jonson had laboured to make
English the tradition which Drummond defended against the
innovators.

James Howell tells about a supper given by Ben Jonson which
he almost spoiled by his efforts 'to magnifie his owne muse'.
Carew complained about this breach of 'good manners'. But
Howell excuses Jonson's failure to exemplify the urbanity of
'Inviting a Friend to Supper': 'But for my part I am content to
dispense with this *Roman* infirmity of *B*. now that time hath
snowed upon his pericranium. You know *Ovid*, and (your)
Horace were subject to this humour.' And then Howell quotes
instances to Sir Thomas Hawkins, the translator of Horace. It is
as if Jonson were entitled to this Roman infirmity along with his
Roman achievements.

This spells out a defect in Jonson that Clarendon only hints at,
but he is more direct about Carew's reputation: 'He was a person
of a pleasant and facetious wit, and made many poems, (especially
in the amorous way,) which for the sharpness of the fancy, and
the elegancy of the language in which that fancy was spread, were
at least equal, if not superior to any of that time.' His virtues
define the influences of Donne and Jonson. But his glory, says
Clarendon, was that he made a religious end. The impulse to such
an end is expressed in his piquant verses 'To Mr. George Sandys':

> *I press not to the choir, nor dare I greet*
> *The holy place with my unhallow'd feet;*
> *My unwash'd Muse pollutes not things divine,*
> *Nor mingles her profaner notes with thine;*
> *Here humbly at the porch she list'ning stays,*
> *And with glad ears sucks in thy sacred lays.*
> *So devout penitents of old were wont,*
> *Some without door and some beneath the font,*
> *To stand and hear the Church's liturgies,*
> *Yet not assist the solemn exercise.*
> *Sufficeth her that she a lay-place gain,*
> *To trim thy vestments, or but bear thy train;*

Though nor in tune nor wing she reach thy lark,
Her lyric feet may dance before the Ark.
Who knows but that her wand'ring eyes, that run
Now hunting glow-worms, may adore the sun?

Having reversed Donne's progress in the lines of 'Elegy XII',

I will not look upon the quickening Sun,
But straight her beauty to my sense shall run;

he proceeds, like Donne, to translate 'sensual love' into divine terms:

Perhaps my restless soul, tir'd with pursuit
Of mortal beauty, seeking without fruit
Contentment there, which hath not, when enjoy'd,
Quench'd all her thirst, nor satisfi'd, though cloy'd,
Weary of her vain search below, above
In the first fair may find th'immortal love.

The syntax is also Donne's. Earlier, in his witty 'Answer of an Elegiacal Letter', he had declared his Muse incapable of the heroic or the sacred:

Alas! how may
My lyric feet, that of the smooth soft way
Of love and beauty only know the tread,
In dancing paces celebrate the dead
Victorious king, or his majestic hearse
Profane with th'humble touch of their low verse?

This is where Carew began the pursuit of beauty which ended, like Donne's, by being translated into higher terms and by contributing power to his fine lines to Sandys.

To Clarendon's praise of Carew we may add his report of a present rival, Waller: 'There needs no more be said to extol the excellence and power of his wit, and pleasantness of his conversation, than that it was of magnitude enough to cover a world of very great faults . . . and continued to his age with that rare felicity, that his company was acceptable, where his spirit was odious.' The merits of this pair were compared by Henry Headley in the eighteenth century as follows: 'Carew has the ease without the pedantry of Waller, and perhaps less conceit. . . . Though Love had long before softened us into civility, yet it was of a formal, ostentatious, and romantic cast; and, with a very few exceptions, its effects upon composition were similar to those on manners. Something more light, unaffected, and alluring, was still wanting; in every thing but sincerity of intention it was deficient. . . . Carew and Waller jointly began to remedy these defects. In them, gallantry, for the first time, was accompanied by the Graces, the fulsomeness of panegyric forgot in its gentility, and the edge of satire rendered keener in proportion to its smoothness.'[1] These are the rivals of 'easy Suckling', and rivals with a better claim to having added grace to gallantry, and with better manners than Jonson. If Jonson developed the mythological mode of compliment, these poets brought it to perfection, though with some pedantry on the part of Waller. Of the latter Rochester said in his *Allusion to Horace*:

> *He best can turn, enforce, and soften things,*
> *To praise great Conquerors, or to flatter Kings.*

Suckling has described the difference between Carew and himself in a poem 'Upon my Lady Carlisle's walking in Hampton Court Garden'.

> Tom. *Didst thou not find the place inspir'd,*
> *And flowers, as if they had desir'd*
> *No other sun, start from their beds,*
> *And for a sight steal out their heads?*
> *Heard'st thou not music when she talk'd?*
> *And didst not find that as she walk'd*
> *She threw rare perfumes all about,*
> *Such as bean-blossoms newly out,*
> *Or chafed spices give?——*

> J.S. *I must confess those perfumes, Tom,*
> *I did not smell; nor found that from*
> *Her passing by aught sprung up new:*
> *The flow'rs had all their birth from you;*

[1] See *Select Beauties of Ancient English Poetry*, London, 1787.

> *For I pass'd o'er the selfsame walk,*
> *And did not find one single stalk*
> *Of any thing that was to bring*
> *This unknown after-after-Spring.*

TOM. *Dull and insensible, couldst see*
> *A thing so near a deity*
> *Move up and down, and feel no change?*

J.S. *None and so great were alike strange.*
> *I had my thoughts, but not your way;*
> *All are not born, sir, to the bay;*
> *Alas! Tom, I am flesh and blood,*
> *And was consulting how I could*
> *In spite of masks and hoods descry*
> *The parts deni'd unto the eye:*
> *I was undoing all she wore;*
> *And had she walk'd but one turn more,*
> *Eve in her first state had not been*
> *More naked, or more plainly seen.*

TOM. *'Twas well for thee she left the place;*
> *There is great danger in that face;*
> *But hadst thou view'd her leg and thigh,*
> *And upon that discovery*
> *Search'd after parts that are more dear*
> *(As fancy seldom stops so near),*
> *No time or age had ever seen*
> *So lost a thing as thou hadst been.*

Obviously these roles mock different modes in which fancy could address the fair, and Suckling does not write in the mode of Waller, which may be compared in his poem on 'The Countess of Carlisle in Mourning'. If we prefer the wit of Suckling, at the close of the seventeenth century Waller was renowned for his happiness 'in raising modern Compliments upon ancient Story, and setting off the British Valour and the English Beauty, with the old Gods and Goddesses.' Their return had been predicted by Carew.

Though Carew was attracted, with Donne, 'From country grass

to comfitures of Court, / Or city's *quelque-choses*', he never forgot
with Jonson either that 'Beautie be the Marke of praise' or that
her finest compliments come from 'Rich Nature's store, which is
the poet's treasure'. His gallantry can give complaint itself the
form of compliment, as in 'A Divine Mistress'.

> *In Nature's pieces still I see*
> *Some error that might mended be;*
> *Something my wish could still remove,*
> *Alter or add; but my fair love*
> *Was fram'd by hands far more divine,*
> *For she hath every beauteous line:*
> *Yet I had been far happier,*
> *Had Nature, that made me, made her.*
> *Then likeness might (that love creates)*
> *Have made her love what now she hates;*
> *Yet, I confess, I cannot spare*
> *From her just shape the smallest hair;*
> *Nor need I beg from all the store*
> *Of heaven for her one beauty more.*
> *She hath too much divinity for me:*
> *You gods, teach her some more humanity.*

But the compliment is pointed or edged, not unexpectedly, by its
paradoxical close. Indeed, Carew's urbane wit is often turned into
ironic gallantry.

Perhaps the supreme example of this form of wit, which extends what Puttenham called dissimulation, is 'The Exequy' by
Henry King. The first lines suggest that grief is to be disguised as
complaint:

> *Accept thou Shrine of my dead Saint,*
> *Instead of Dirges this complaint.*

Instead of the usual song of mourning we are to hear a complaint
'from thy griev'd friend', a tender expression of grievance; the
ambiguity of 'grieve' fixes the complexity of tone. Thus his elegy
is touched with just enough wit to avoid any suggestion of the
mawkish.

The effect of her death is first expressed in terms of the studious routine which it upsets. The wit of complaint turns his weeping into an effect of blindness as he tries to read, and then of measuring time by wet hour-glasses—or metaphors in which ingenuity merges into reticence.

Indeed, her loss has reversed time for him:

> *Nor wonder if my time go thus*
> *Backward and most preposterous.*

Here 'preposterous' Latinizes 'backward' and adds the meaning of 'absurd'. The effect is to lighten the solemnity of his predicament as he begins to particularize his tender complaint. Her 'untimely fate' makes time a basic element of their separation and of his unhappiness. As his sun, another measure of time, her departure introduces other images of separation. This he could allow if the separation were limited, but unfortunately it must last until Doomesday.

Meanwhile the earth has her, and so he directs his complaint to the earth, which he threatens with a strict accounting of its trust. Then her burial or funeral bed takes on the ambiguity of marriage bed, and King fashions his own version of Marvell's theme,

> *The Grave's a fine and private place,*
> *But none I think do there embrace.*

Each night carries him closer to his eventual rendezvous with her; his journey now takes on the semblance of a voyage. Then it assumes a military form as he again chides her—this time for dying before him.

The thought that he will finally overtake her, gives him the courage to go on,

> *And wait my dissolution*
> *With hope and comfort.*

Though his resolve is a crime towards her, it is on his part an act of Christian resignation. Thus a funeral procession is extended in various guises and with various feelings until the ultimate meeting of Doomesday.

In theory the wit derived from mythology is viewed less favourably by Sir Thomas Browne than by Drummond, but on other grounds. In Book I of his *Vulgar Errors* (1646) he deals with the causes of common errors, and in Chapter IX considers the poets, who have contributed by using popular errors in their similes. This is the 'occasion of error unto vulgar heads, who expect in the fable as equal a truth as in the moral', although 'wiser discerners do well understand that every art hath its own circle', and strict expression is not always required. The hieroglyphics of the Egyptians escaped this shortcoming: 'For, using an alphabet of things, and not of words, through the image and pictures thereof they endeavoured to speak their hidden conceits in the letters and language of nature.' Since men are brought up on mythological fictions or allusions, they later drive 'at these as at the highest elegancies, which are but the frigidities of wit, and become not the genius of manly ingenuities.' After condemning this kind of wit, Browne makes a suggestion which would have pleased Greville earlier and Sprat later: 'For, were a pregnant wit educated in ignorance hereof, receiving only impressions from realities, upon such solid foundations, it must surely raise more substantial superstructions, and fall upon very many excellent strains, which have been justled off by their intrusions'. And this would have pleased Carew far more than Drummond, but in general it points away from both. They would have been much more sympathetic to Hoskins' view of metaphor: 'Besides, a metaphor is pleasant because it enricheth our knowledge with two things at once, with the truth and with similitude.' Browne, on the other hand, was anticipating Sprat's requirements for wit.

* 2 *

The relations of metre and rhetoric are involved in the use of wit in this time, and hence deserve some attention. The Renaissance quarrel between the native and the classical tradition in verse centred in rhyme and its potentialities. In its last phase this quarrel reduced itself to the opposition between stopped verse and run-on verse, for these were crucial urgencies of the two systems.[1]

[1] See J. V. Cunningham, 'Classical and Medieval,' *Tradition and Poetic Structure*, Denver, 1960.

Ben Jonson in his *Conversations with Drummond* expressed his preference for couplets, and 'Said he had written a discourse of poesy both against Campion and Daniel, especially this last, where he proves couplets to be the bravest sort of verses, especially when they are broken, like hexameters; and that cross rhymes and stanzas (because the purpose would lead him beyond eight lines to conclude) were all forced.' The parenthesis explains why 'Spenser's stanzas pleased him not' and why he disliked Petrarch's sonnet. In his own stanzas Jonson is chary of cross rhymes or internal complication. Donne made his stanzas emphasize or point the rhetoric of a more complicated syntax.

Daniel had held that 'those continual cadences of couplets used in long and continued Poems, are very tiresome, and unpleasing'; he preferred 'sometimes to beguile the ear, with a running out, and passing over the Rhyme.' Jonson replied, 'Some loved running verses, *plus mihi comma placet.*' He emphasized his preference for stopped verses in his censure of Drummond's verses: 'that they smelled too much of the Schools, and were not after the fancy of the time; for a child, says he, may write after the fashion of the Greeks and Latin verses in running.'

For this fashion we may turn to Milton's note on the verse of *Paradise Lost*: 'The measure is *English* Heroic Verse without Rime, as that of *Homer* in *Greek*, and of *Virgil* in *Latin*; Rime being no necessary Adjunct or true Ornament of Poem or good Verse, in longer Works especially, but the Invention of a barbarous Age, to set off wretched matter and lame Meeter . . . a thing of it self, to all judicious eares, triveal and of no true musical delight; which consists only in apt Numbers, fit quantity of Syllables, and the sense variously drawn out from one Verse into another.' Milton's position is the very opposite of Jonson's, and emphasizes what Jonson calls 'verses in running'. Jonson clearly elects the most restricted form of couplet, broken by the caesura, stopped by the comma; and this is the form which he established in his *Epigrams*, the ripest of his studies.

These were different ways of escaping from the tyranny of the Spenserian stanza, or the stanzaic tradition of the Spenserians. The stanza as used by Donne developed from the pattern of his thought, and then served to emphasize or point the rhetoric of his sentence. He created emergent stanza forms to fit his more complicated syntax, or suspended it more freely over the sonnet form. But he did not loosen that form to the extent that Milton did, or imitate forms of the ode.

Sir John Beaumont in his verses 'Concerning the true forme of English Poetry' (1629) echoes the contemporary doctrine of Jonson on couplets:

> *Their forme surpassing farre the fetter'd staves,*
> *Vaine care, and needlesse repetition saves.*

His ideas on diction extend the parallel:

> *Pure phrase, fit Epithets, a sober care*
> *Of Metaphors, descriptions cleare, yet rare,*
> *Similitudes contracted smooth and round,*
> *Not vext by learning, but with Nature crown'd.*

Similitudes have to be compressed for couplets—as they slowly learned. Beaumont differs from Hoskins by rejecting learning in favour of nature as a source of wit; he is Jonsonian in his notion of strength:

> *Strong figures drawne from deepe inventions springs,*
> *Consisting lesse in words, and more in things.*

If Jonson disliked Spenser's archaic language, Beaumont requires

> *A language not affecting ancient times,*
> *Nor Latine shreds, by which the Pedant climes.*

He is likewise against 'darksome words' or

> *envious muses, which sad garlands wear*
> *Of dusky clouds, their strange conceits to hide.*

Both compression and Oedipean conceits could produce the obscurity which they stigmatized in 'strong lines'. But Jonson observed, among the differences of wits, that 'rough and broken' composition was likewise associated with the 'strong and manly'.

In 1640 a minor poet explains his couplets 'To the Reader' as follows: 'For the verses, I have kept to one number and measure, only the *Epitaphs* are woven stanzas: In a continued subject, it is not proper to vary the verse. I have laboured to make the lines so smooth as I could, in placing the breathing accents where they may fall with most advantage, (except those which run cleane without them) nor have I broke the first, or last foot of the verse, which might make it run harsh, nor straind the coupling accents above what is required in the harmony: nor fallen too low in the descent, which might give the verse an unnaturall sound, where the concords should chiefly meet.'[1] It is evident that the care for smoothness depends largely upon the management of the caesura and of rhyme, but Mill also instructs the reader in the ways in which pronunciation may affect the number of syllables in any verse. This must have been a common view when Waller decided that English verses 'want smoothness, and began to essay'.

In establishing the couplet in his *Epigrams* Jonson also explored the modes of thought and feeling which had been cultivated by the Epigram, especially in Martial: wit, satire, compliment, funeral pathos, statement of moral truths, sharply etched characters, set off by the elegance of the form, sometimes by contrast between matter and form. Thus the epigrammatic norm of the couplet endowed the couplet with its characteristic modes of thought and feeling as well as its more obvious form. The combination of elegance and elegiac pathos also appears in other metres in Jonson's famous epitaphs, but the epigrammatic quality persists in a kind of elegant and polite reticence in grief.

Since the wit of epigram shows a fondness for double meanings and forms of contradiction (paradox, antithesis, irony), point and antithesis and paradox were much cultivated. The wit of opposition was most effective in moulding the couplet because of the impulse toward parallel structure and balance which it brought with it. In Jonson's *Epigrams* the stopped couplet and antithetic rhetoric are unusually prevalent; in his other couplet verses the antithetic rhetoric is much less common, and the couplets are much more inclined to run on. Stopped first lines—a later step in

---

[1] Humphrey Mill, *A Nights Search*, London, 1640.

the evolution of the Neo-classical couplet—are also more common in the couplets of the *Epigrams*. Altogether, the correspondence of metre and rhetoric is more observable in these verses than in Jonson's epistolary couplets.

Another impulse towards this form may be found in Ovidian rhetoric and metre. In an old *History of Roman Literature* (1877) by C. T. Cruttwell, we find a recognition of this possibility in a discussion of parallelism in Virgil: 'This feature in Virgil's verse, which might be illustrated at far greater length, reappears under another form in the Ovidian elegiac. There the pentameter answers to the second half of Virgil's hexameter verse, and rings the changes on the line that has preceded in a very similar way. A literature which loves the balanced clauses of rhetoric will be sure to have something analogous. Our own heroic couplet is a case in point. So perhaps is the invention of rhyme which tends to confine the thought within the oscillating limits of a refrain.' Thus where Virgil balances half-line against half-line, Ovid puts line against line, and adds various kinds of correspondence. The wit of contradiction which animates this Ovidian form became the final target of Dryden's efforts to define the proper wit of poetry even as he recognized the imitation of this form in Sandys.

IV

INTERREGNUM WIT

In 'The Chronicle', when the reigns of his supposed mistresses are interrupted, Cowley's wit connects politics and poetry:

> But in her place I then Obey'd
> Black-ey'd Bess her Vice-Roy Maid,
> To whom ensu'd a Vacancy.
> Thousand worse Passions then possest
> The Inter-regnum of my Breast.
> Bless me from such an Anarchy!

During the Interregnum of wit the rhetoric of disparity comes into increasing prominence. We saw its forms in Hoskins, and we find them neatly grouped under *dissimilitudes* in Obadiah Walker's *Some Instructions concerning the Art of Oratory* (1659): 'Dissimilitudes, or Comparisons with, and Illustrations by Contraries.' These 'Dissimilitudes are expressed, either by *Disjunction* [as in antithesis] . . . Or by *Commutation* and *Inversion* and several wayes of comparing together, and reflecting upon them [as in *antimetabole*] . . . Or by denominating them also one of another [as in *oxymoron* or paradox].' On the latter he comments like Hoskins: 'Which because commonly not done without strength of fancy in the Orator, is the more remarked and admired by the Auditor, much taken to see opposites agree and contradictions true.'

Walker illustrates this wit from Ovid where Dryden later condemned it:

> Now, in that mine, not mine: Proximity
> Dis-joyns us: nearer, were we not so nigh.

As Sidney admitted, this part of rhetoric, 'this wordish considera-
tion', is shared by poetry too. These forms capitalize on surprise
and the shock of contrasted feeling. The wit of antimetabole, for
example, is exhibited with virtuosity in Denham's *Cooper's Hill*.
On the use of fancy Walker offers this advice: 'In inventing take
heed of torturing your fancy too much at first; either in the quest
of more curious matter, or in setting it down in the most exact
form. For, besides that the mind doth more heavily and less
accurately, perform many things at once; the Wit especially, is
of so delicate a sharpness, that any forcing presently turns the
edge.' Fancy or Wit is the faculty of invention throughout his
rhetoric.

Several new incentives to the 'torturing' of fancy seem to have
been operative at this time. Great admiration of Lucan is evident
in various ways. John Hall, the poet, translates Longinus as *The
Height of Eloquence* (1652). Meric Casaubon in his *Treatise of
Enthusiasme* (1655) relates 'strong lines' to Longinus on bombast,
or the extremity of style that Dryden calls 'Clevelandism' and
that Gilbert Burnet later calls 'a wrong sublime'. This is the other
side of what Burnet describes as 'the coarse extravagance of
Canting'; in poetry it is legitimized as 'Pindarics'.

Among the eulogists of Cartwright's *Poems* (1651) one observes
two divergent tendencies. One is to praise him for his judgment,
as in the line by John Berkenhead afterwards made famous
by Dryden: 'For the great Wit's great work is to Refuse.' The
other and chief tendency is to praise him for his wit. Though
Jasper Mayne feels that he writes in 'Times which make it Treason
to be witty', he falls into this vein in saluting Cartwright:

> *Hence twin perfections in thy Writings knit,*
> *Present us with strange Contraries of Wit:*
> *Strength mix'd with Sweetness, Vigorous, with Fair;*
> *Lucan's bold Heights match'd to staid Virgil's care,*
> *Martial's quick salt, joind to Musaeus Tongue,*
> *Soft thorns of Fancie which from Roses sprung.*
> *Thou hadst, indeed, a sharp but harmless Wit;*
> *Made to delight, and please, not wound, or hit:*

INTERREGNUM WIT

A Wit which was all Edge, yet none did feel
Rasours in thy quick Line, in thy Verse steel;
Or if they did, only from thence did spring
A pointed Musick, sharpness without sting.

This is text enough for what has been said, especially as it comes together in a wit of contradiction. In general the eulogists, like Mayne, feel rebellious against the 'Levellers of Wit', and this feeling may have strengthened an impulse towards extravagance that is found in poets of the Interregnum.

The re-definition of wit was undertaken by Davenant in his 'Preface to Gondibert'. This preface stimulated Hobbes to a more precise statement based on his own psychology. Where the old identification of wit and wisdom seems to operate at times in Davenant, Hobbes is more careful to make distinctions; but on many points they agree, and not least on the state of wit at this time. Indeed, they reflect the old ideas and begin to articulate the new.

Davenant observes, 'That if any Disciples of unimitable *Virgil* can prove so formal as to esteem wit (as if it were levity) an imputation to the Heroick Muse (by which malevolent word, Wit, they would disgrace her extraordinary heights)' they will have to be content to have 'few of their society'. This describes exactly the later position of Addison on wit and heroic poetry. Davenant remarks of Lucan, 'And now I will leave to others the presumption of measuring his Hyperboles, by whose space and height they maliciously take the dimension of wit.' These might be the criteria of wit for Donne's 'Valediction: of the book'. They do suggest the grounds on which Dryden passed from the admiration to the renunciation of Lucan.

Yet Davenant's ambition to pitch his epic lower, closer to drama, might have led him to renounce such wit. He criticizes Virgil as he might have criticized Milton for taking us 'where Nature never comes, even into Heaven and Hell . . . till by conversation with Gods and Ghosts he sometimes deprives us of those natural probabilities in Story which are instructive to humane life'. Here he is asserting a criterion that is to become fundamental in the new esthetics.

Davenant uses the basic metaphor of a house to organize his discussion, and comes to wit when he arrives at furniture. Of his 'ornaments or Hangings' he says, 'yet I shall not give you the trouble of inquiring what is, but tell you of what I design'd, their substance, which is, *Wit*: And *Wit* is the laborious and the lucky resultances of thought, having towards its excellence, as we say of the strokes of Painting, as well a happinesse as care. . . . *Wit* is not only the luck and labour, but also the dexterity of thought, rounding the world, like the Sun, with unimaginable motion, and bringing swiftly home to the memory universall surveys. It is the Souls *Powder*, which when supprest, as forbidden from flying upward, blows up the restraint, and loseth all force in a farther ascension towards Heaven.' This passage stimulated Hobbes to his own explanation of the dexterity of fancy, and possibly to the need for restraint. But it is also well to remember that for Davenant poems are furnished by ornament and the substance of that ornament is wit. All of this helps us to understand Hobbes, if not, as Davenant suggested, to define wit.

Davenant is more helpful in telling us what is outmoded in wit. Young men, he says, 'imagine it consists in the Musick of words, and beleeve they are made wise by refining their Speech above the vulgar Dialect. . . . From the esteem of speaking they proceed to the admiration of what are commonly call'd *Conceits*, things that sound like the knacks or toyes of ordinary *Epigrammatists*, and from thence, after more conversation and variety of objects, grow up to some force of Fancy.' His remarks about old men annoyed Hobbes, but are less significant for us, except for this remark: 'Old men, that have forgot their first Childhood and are returning to their second, think it lyes in *agnominations*, and in a kinde of an alike tinkling of words.' Their infatuation with sound effects has a rhetorical name and associates their taste with the Euphuistic past.

Davenant's most illuminating comment on wit summarizes his own ambition: 'Nor will I presume to call the matter of which the Ornaments or Substantial parts of this Poem are compos'd, *Wit*; but onely tell you my endeavour was, in bringing Truth, too often absent, home to mens bosoms, to lead her through unfrequented

and new ways, and from the most remote Shades, by representing
Nature, though not in an affected, yet in an unusual dress.' Thus
truth is to be made effective by the expression, wit is to make it
new. But lest we misunderstand both Davenant and Hobbes, let
us note that he is talking about 'the matter of which the Ornaments or Substantial parts of this Poem are composed', and hence
that the 'unusual dress' is indeed the substance of the poem. We
should beware of giving a superficial sense to ornament in their
discussion, since it involves representation.

For Hobbes too fancy is related to quickness of mind. In
Human Nature (chapter X) he speaks of this quickness 'which is
joyned with *Curiosity* of comparing the Things that come into the
Mind, one with another: in which Comparison, a Man delighteth
himself either with finding unexpected *Similitude* of Things, otherwise much unlike, in which Men place the Excellency of *Fancy*,
and from whence proceed those grateful Similes, Metaphors, and
other Tropes, by which both *Poets* and *Orators* have it in their
Power to make Things please or displease, and shew well or ill
to others, as they like themselves; or else in discerning suddenly
Dissimilitude in Things that otherwise appear the same. And this
Vertue of the Mind is that by which Men attain to exact and perfect *Knowledge*; and the Pleasure thereof consisteth in continual
Instruction, and in Distinction of Places, Persons, and Seasons,
and is commonly termed by the Name of Judgement, for, to
judge is nothing else, but to distinguish or discern.' Here we may
note that men place the excellency of Fancy in finding unexpected
similitude in things otherwise much unlike, and we should also
note that judgment leads both to knowledge and to propriety.

But quickness of mind may have another consequence for
Hobbes that is related to our subject, not only because it threatens
propriety: 'There is another Defect of the Mind, which Men call
Levity, which betrayeth also *Mobility* in the Spirits, but in Excess.
An Example whereof is in them that in the midst of any serious
Discourse, have their Minds diverted to every little Jest or witty
Observation; which maketh them depart from their Discourse by
a Parenthesis, and from that Parenthesis by another, till at length
they either lose themselves, or make their Narration like a Dream,

or some studied Nonsence. The Passion from whence this proceedeth, is *Curiosity*, but with *too much Equality* and Indifference: for when all Things make equal Impression and Delight, they equally throng to be expressed.' Hence quickness of mind in excess produces levity, which is associated with jest; and when Hobbes treats jest (chapter IX) he says that to move laughter 'it must be *new* and *unexpected.*' Thus we may discover the difficulty of distinguishing between serious wit and facetious wit, of which Davenant took notice.

Of course this is an earlier stage of the analysis we find in the *Leviathan*. There he is separating fancy from the wits that may properly be called intellectual virtues or excellences, and so he is at pains to say that what is called a 'Good Wit' is really a 'Good Fancy'. In this context the relations between fancy and judgment are developed, and judgment becomes necessary to a good fancy in order to avoid levity or an excess of quickness or fancy. In the *Leviathan* Hobbes is saying that what is called a good fancy may err in propriety, but good judgment can never be less than an intellectual virtue. The insistence on judgment does not displace fancy from its eminence in poetry, but it does limit it, and the ultimate criterion of this limitation is Nature, or the knowledge of nature. This criterion establishes the importance of judgment.

In the famous passage in his 'Answer to Davenant' this relation is crucial to our understanding: 'Memory begets Judgement and Fancy; Judgment begets the strength and structure, and Fancy begets the ornaments of a Poem.' Hobbes explains how judgment orders memory or experience into knowledge, and so provides materials for the creations of fancy or the compounding imagination. But 'the workmanship of Fancy' must be guided by 'the Precepts of true Philosophy' or knowledge. Where these precepts fail, 'as they have hitherto failed in the doctrine of moral vertue, there the Architect, Fancy, must take the Philosophers part upon her self' and 'furnish and square' her own material; to be a true guide philosophy must not be contentious. Where knowledge is uncertain fancy must provide her own 'strength and structure' in her creations; the architect must be his own engineer. Obviously the 'doctrine of moral virtue' is no small area in poetry.

Having laid down the criterion of resemblance to nature for
expression too, Hobbes continues: 'That which giveth a Poem the
true and natural Colour consisteth in two things, which are, *To
know well*, that is, to have images of nature in the memory distinct
and clear, and *To know much*. A signe of the first is perspicuity,
property, and decency, which delight all sorts of men, either by
instructing the ignorant or soothing the learned in their knowledge. A signe of the latter is novelty of expression, and pleaseth
by excitation of the minde; for novelty causeth admiration, and
admiration curiosity, which is a delightful appetite of knowledge.'
The bases of these virtues should be noted well and their relation
to the faculties of judgment and fancy. A defect in knowing well
which becomes a failure in perspicuity is illustrated by 'strong
lines': 'To this palpable darkness [hard words] I may also add
the ambitious obscurity of expressing more then is perfectly conceived, or perfect conception in fewer words then it requires.'

But his comment on the relation of fancy to knowledge is closer
to Davenant's discussion of wit: 'From *Knowing much*, proceedeth
the admirable variety and novelty of Metaphors and Similitudes,
which are not possible to be lighted on in the compass of a narrow
knowledge. And the want whereof compelleth a Writer to expressions that are either defac'd by time or sullied with vulgar or long
use. For the Phrases of Poesy, as the airs of musick, with often
hearing become insipide, the Reader having no more sense of their
force then our Flesh is sensible of the Bones that sustain it. As the
sense we have of bodies consisteth in change and variety of impression, so also does the sense of language in the variety and
changeable use of words. I mean not in the affectation of words
newly brought home from travail, but in new and with all significant translation to our purposes of those that be already
received, and in far fetch't but withal apt, instructive, and comly
similitudes.' Thus Hobbes provides the theoretical basis for
Davenant's endeavour to convey truth 'through unfrequented
and new ways, and from the most remote Shades, by representing Nature, though not in an affected, yet in an unusual dress'.
Hobbes' phrase, 'far fetch't but withal apt', bridges the gap that
will only grow wider because of his theory. Yet the relation of

good fancy to breadth of knowledge provides the theory for the older practice of wit, as in Donne, and emphasizes again the importance of the matter as well as the form of wit, and even to the form of wit. Benlowes in his preface to *Theophila* has made a conflation of ideas found in *Human Nature* and the 'Answer to Davenant'.

Gondibert also had two poets as sponsors, Cowley and Waller; and Cowley was interested in the theory as well as practice of wit. He begins his eulogy of *Gondibert* with these lines:

> *Me thinks Heroick Poesie till now,*
> *Like some fantastick Fairy-land did show;*
> *Gods, Devils, Nymphs, Witches, and Giants race,*
> *And all but Man, in Mans best work had place.*

This deliberately points to Davenant's banishment of the supernatural in favour of the natural in the epic, and hence has an occasional motive. But in 1656 in a note to his Pindaric ode, 'The Muse', Cowley emphasizes poetic license: '*Whatsoever God made*; for his saying, *Let it be*, made all Things. The meaning is, that Poetry treats not only of all Things that are, or can be, but makes Creatures of her own, as Centaurs, Satyrs, Fairies, &c., makes Persons and Actions of her own, as in Fables and Romances; makes Beasts, Trees, Waters, and other irrational and insensible Things to act above the Possibility of their Natures, as to understand and speak; nay makes what Gods it pleases too without Idolatry, and varies all these into innumerable Systemes, or Worlds of Invention.' Hobbes had said that the poet was not to go 'beyond the conceived possibility of nature'.

In his 'Ode: Of Wit' Cowley takes a more rhetorical approach to wit. He remarks that nothing loves variety more, and in nothing does London deceive us more. Like Davenant and Hobbes, he rules out levity as wit. 'The *Proofs* of *Wit* for ever must remain': this is Dryden's test in the *Essay of Dramatic Poesy*. Wit is not the power of numbers; not ornament, but this is closer. 'Rather than *all things Wit*, let *none* be there.' Nor is it puns:

> *In which who finds out* Wit, *the same may see*
> *In* An'grams *and* Acrostiques Poetry.

This is before *Mac Flecknoe*. There follows the famous exclusion of anything 'At which a *Virgin* hides her Face'. He then makes a list of outmoded wit: it is not strong lines, tall metaphor, or bombast, nor Senecan epigram, nor 'odd Similitude'. It is not so much a *discordia concors* as a harmony of all. The end comes back to the *variety* of the beginning—and of Hobbes—but not before it has rejected several kinds of wit. Cowley's 'Answer to a Copy of Verses sent me to Jersey' celebrates the lack of rhetorical wit in Jersey. Metaphor is unknown, and there are no clinches: 'Which shows the People have *Judgment*, if not *Wit*.' They are so far from bombast that they lack even the first impulse towards strong lines. The 'Answer' merely emphasizes some of the rejections of the 'Ode'.

By 1661 the limitation of fancy had gone farther in Cowley's thinking. In his Preface to *A Proposition for the Advancement of Experimental Philosophy* he says: 'Our Reasoning Faculty as well as Fancy, does but Dream, when it is not guided by sensible Objects. We shall compound where Nature has divided, and divide where Nature has compounded, and create nothing but either Deformed Monsters, or at best pretty but impossible Mermaids. 'Tis like Painting by Memory and Imagination which can never produce a Picture to the Life.' Thinking of one of Bacon's projects, he deplores the lack of poets who have treated 'Natural Matters (the most part indulging to the weakness of the world, and feeding it either with the follies of Love, or with the Fables of gods and Heroes).' In his 'Answer to Davenant', however, Hobbes had said that 'natural causes' were not the province of poets.

In his *Proposition* Cowley is associating himself with Baconian thought, and his position may be clarified by comparing his views with those of Bacon. In *The Advancement of Learning* Bacon had begun by enumerating the vanities in studies. After the 'vain words' of the Ciceronians he had deplored the 'vain matter' of the Schoolmen, especially for this reason: 'For the wit and mind of man, if it work upon matter, which is the contemplation of the creatures of God, worketh according to the stuff, and is limited thereby; but if it work upon itself, as the spider worketh his web, then it is endless, and brings forth indeed cobwebs of learning, admirable for the fineness of thread and work, but of no substance or profit.' Cowley said in his Preface that the Schoolmen did not 'so much as touch Nature, because they catcht only at the shadow of her in their own Brains'. Bacon tried to turn the mind from notional philosophy to empirical philosophy, or towards knowledge that is not independent of sense perception.

But in his efforts towards a re-orientation of the mind Bacon did not go as far as Cowley. Bacon, like Sidney, left imagination and poetry free, not limited like philosophy and history: 'Poesy is a part of Learning in measure of words for the most part restrained, but in all other points extremely licensed, and doth truly refer to the imagination, which, being not tied to the laws of matter, may at pleasure join that which Nature hath severed, and sever that which Nature hath joined, and so make unlawful matches and divorces of things . . . it doth raise and erect the mind, by submitting the shows of things to the desires of the mind, whereas reason doth buckle and bow the mind unto the nature of things.' Bacon does not, like Cowley, limit both imagination and reason 'unto the nature of things'. To do so would frustrate the end of poetry: 'The use of this Feigned History hath been to give some shadow of satisfaction to the mind of man in those points wherein the nature of things doth deny it, the world being in proportion inferior to the soul.' Reality cannot satisfy man's craving for proportion or the ideal.

Perhaps the explanation of the difference between Cowley and Bacon is to be found in Hobbes. In the *Leviathan* (1651) Hobbes speaks of the compounding imagination in terms similar to those of Bacon. Opposed to the simple image is another: 'The other is *Compounded*; as when from the sight of a man at one time, and of a horse at another, we conceive in our mind a Centaure. So when a man compoundeth the image of his own person, with the image of the actions of an other man; as when a man imagins himselfe a *Hercules*, or an *Alexander*, (which happeneth often to them that are much taken with reading of Romants) it is a compound imagination, and properly but a Fiction of the mind.' Simple imagination (as decaying sense images) reproduces nature; compounding imagination produces new combinations of nature. But in his 'Answer to Davenant' Hobbes had already limited the fancy or fiction of poetry with respect to Nature. 'There are some', he complained, 'that are not pleased with fiction, unless it be bold, not onely to exceed the *work*, but also the *possibility* of nature.'

Then he extends Bacon's criterion of history to poetry or feigned history: 'For as truth is the bound of Historical, so the Resemblance of truth is the utmost limit of Poeticall Liberty. In old time amongst the Heathen such strange fictions and Metamorphoses were not so remote from the Articles of their Faith as they are now from ours, and therefore were not so unpleasant. Beyond the actual works of nature a Poet may now go; but beyond the conceived possibility of nature, never.' From this limitation of the imagination Dryden will find his escape in some 'articles of faith'. Now Hobbes sets up a similar criterion for expression, which 'shews well or ill, as it hath more or less resemblance with the natural'. Sprat extends this criterion to the requirements for wit by outlawing the metaphysical and demanding a physical basis of wit. The new criterion for imagination involved judgment, and Nature soon became the important basis of propriety.

* 2 *

In practice the rhetoric of disparity takes on more overt forms. Contrived disparities of various sorts are exploited. Later, not 'a propriety of thoughts and words', but a disparity between style and theme created the mock-heroic and more sophisticated pastorals. Marvell's *Nymph* exploits the naive and sophisticated, but not with the cynicism of the Restoration pastoral. Still it is a more obvious contrast of feeling than that employed in King's *Exequy*. If the disparity between style and subject often nullifies the emotion of Cleveland's love poems, it is a source of power in his satiric wit. Much as with Dryden, Cleveland's high style was never so successful as when it magnified the absurdity of its subject. Indeed, the exemplary wit of this time can be distinguished most clearly in Cleveland and Cowley.

Cleveland's mode of wit is best explained by 'The Hecatomb to

his Mistress', for it begins like his satires although it is a panegyric. And it begins by discriminating his aims and methods from
those of the poetasters:

> *Be dumb you Beggars of the rhyming Trade,*
> *Geld your loose wits, & let your Muse be spade.*
> *Charge not the Parish with your bastard Phrase*
> *Of Balm, Elixir, both the India's,*
> *Of Shrine, Saint, Sacrifice, and such as these,*
> *Expressions common as your Mistresses.*
> *Hence you Phantastick Postillers in Song,*
> *My Text defeats your Art, ties Nature's tongue,*
> *Scorns all her Tinsoyl'd Metaphors of Pelf,*
> *Illustrated by nothing but her self.*

With scorn of the stock sources of metaphor, the poem begins
like his satires in order to introduce novel sources of praise rather
than of ridicule. Occasionally Cleveland caricatures some of the
stock sources, as of anatomy poems in 'Fuscara', or of religious
amplification in 'The Senses Festival'. Here his new way is
pointed by the last line, but it requires ingenuity:

> *From your own Essence must I first untwine,*
> *Then twist again each Panegyrick line.*

By this method Jonson restored mythology in his epigram 'To
Mary Lady Wroth', but Cleveland takes more learning for his
province.

Cleveland draws upon such areas of metaphor as angelology,
music, metals, gems, planets, pure substances, astrology, sensuous
perception, or mathematics. For example, he affects the metaphysics for his lady:

> *As then a purer Substance is defin'd*
> *But by an heap of Negatives combin'd,*

so she,

> *For what Perfection we to others grant,*
> *It is her sole Perfection to want.*

Or he gives her powers of synesthesia or witchcraft:

INTERREGNUM WIT

Sweet Magick, which can make five Senses lie
Conjur'd within the Circle of an Eye!

He enters into competition with

Thou Man of mouth that canst not name a she,
Unless all Nature pay a Subsidy,

and finally confounds learning itself by declaring,

What e'er thou understand'st not say't of her,
For that's the way to write her Character.

Here he suggests the relation of his mode of wit to that of the Character-writers, a form in which he first appeared. This may explain the air of caricature which hangs over his work, even when he meant only to give some vent to his daring strain. In this poem his conclusion recalls his opening challenge: 'Then roll up, Muse, what thou hast ravel'd out.' He touched with caricature various fashions of wit even in poems that have no obvious satiric object. Cleveland showed the way to transform the Metaphysical style to the uses of satiric levity: to set seriousness and levity at odds—as in the mock-heroic—by a deliberate impropriety of words and thoughts; how to deflate by inflation, consciously.

But Cleveland's levity often sophisticates without nullifying more serious feeling. 'The Senses Festival' is not an imitation of the anatomy lesson of Donne's *Elegies* or of Carew's 'Rapture'. It is devoid of sensuality; its wit is lighter, more playful, not committed to passion. Although it may echo Donne's 'Extasie',

When Bodies joyn, and Vict'ry hovers
'Twixt the equal fluttering Lovers,

it concludes with mock military gallantry,

Then have at all, the Pass is got,
For coming off, oh name it not!
Who would not die upon the spot?

This metaphoric innuendo will become less subtle in the Restoration.

75

Cleveland gives a new turn to religious amplification in the first stanza:

> *I saw a Vision yesternight*
> *Enough to sate a Seeker's sight,*
> *I wish'd my self a Shaker there,*
> *And her quick Pants my trembling Sphere.*
> *It was a She so glittering bright,*
> *You'd think her Soul an Adamite,*
> *A Person of so rare a frame,*
> *Her Body might be lin'd with th' same.*
> *Beautie's chiefest Maid of Honour,*
> *You may break Lent with looking on her.*
>> *Not the fair Abbess of the Skies*
>> *With all her Nunnery of Eyes*
>> *Can shew me such a glorious Prize.*

It is almost as if he had said here, 'have it in the Saints Gibbrish', or 'the Idiom of the Saints', but the line about Lent is pure Cleveland. Yet his flippant allusions do not diminish her attraction but rather augment her charms.

Likewise Cleveland gives a new turn to geographical metaphor:

> *Is not the Universe strait lac'd,*
> *When I can clasp it in the Waste?*
> *My amorous Fold about thee hurl'd,*
> *With Drake I girdle in the World;*
> *I hoop the Firmament, and make*
> *This my Embrace the Zodiack.*

Waller's 'On a Girdle' plays upon a similar figure without the heroic wit. Cleveland's images often do become poetry though qualified by levity, and merit Dryden's defence of his own, that they 'will still be poetry when the merry fit is over'.

Cleveland in dead earnest, touched with sardonic wit, may be heard in his 'Epitaph on the Earl of Strafford':

> *Here lies wise and valiant dust,*
> *Huddled up 'twixt fit and juste:*
> *Strafford, who was hurried hence*
> *'Twixt treason and convenience.*

He spent his time here in a mist,
A Papist, yet a Calvinist;
His Prince's nearest joy and Grief:
He had, yet wanted, all relief:
The Prop and Ruine of the State,
The peoples violent love and hate.
One in extremes lov'd and abhorr'd.
Riddles lie here, or in a word,
Here lies blood, and let it lie
Speechlesse still, and never cry.

This epitaph develops a series of contradictions in Strafford and his fate. The extremes of feeling involved add to its power, and the condensation adds to the riddling quality of the feeling expressed. The conclusion,

Here lies blood, and let it lie
Speechlesse still, and never cry,

is strong in innuendo, for its iteration plays upon the old belief that blood will cry out ('murder will out') but also suggests resignation, or an act of oblivion.

In his prose Cleveland expresses the same complex attitude towards Strafford. In a defence of a defence of Strafford, he remarks: 'Because it shows wherein the same Man may both condemn and acquit the same Man. Why, is that such a Riddle?' And on another occasion he says that Strafford may be 'both at once Condemn'd and Sav'd'. The extremes in the epitaph are pointed or edged, even to the conclusion, by the wit of contradiction, which involves the King.

Another example of riddling elegiac epigram is Jonson's 'Epitaph on Elizabeth, L.H'. His one epitaph in the enigmatic vein also continues to tantalize the imagination. After praising her in succinct hyperbole, Jonson concludes:

If, at all, she had a fault,
Leave it buried in this vault.
One name was Elizabeth,
Th' other let it sleep with death:

INTERREGNUM WIT

Fitter, where it dyed to tell,
Than that it liv'd at all. Farewell.

As with Strafford, the suggestion of fault adds mystery to her memory. In neither case is it easy to 'let it sleep with death'.

A novel style of elegiac wit is found in Milton's epitaphs 'On the University Carrier', but it is not a style that Cleveland employed, even in his elegy on Edward King. These epitaphs might persuade us that Hobson died of puns, rather facetiously; certainly they make it easier to defend the taste of Cleveland's elegy on King, since his elegiac wit does not belittle. These epitaphs may be compared with John Hoskins' epigram in this vein:

> *Here lies Tom Short, the king of good fellows,*
> *Who in his time was a mender of bellows,*
> *But when he came to the hour of his death,*
> *He that made bellows could not make breath.*

Or this one in a satirical vein:

> *Here lies Gresham under the ground,*
> *As wise as fifty thousand pound;*
> *He never refused the drink of his friend,*
> *Drink was his life and drunk was his end.*

Marvell, although capable of such wit, had a surer sense of decorum than Milton. In his *Rehearsal Transprosed* (Part II) he could 'speak of Hudibras, with that esteem which an excellent piece of wit upon whatsoever subject will always merit' and then defend Milton: 'It was his misfortune, living in a tumultuous time, to be tossed on the wrong side, and he writ *flagrante bello* certain dangerous treatises. . . . At his Majesties happy return, J.M. did partake, even as you yourself did for all your huffing, of his regal clemency, and has ever since expiated himself in a retired silence.' For all his decency, Marvell's wit did not forget to sting Parker in the last sentence.

Cowley, as Dryden recognized, was the greatest explorer or creator of different varieties of wit in his time. Just as Cowley's 'Ode: Of Wit' was the most influential definition of wit, so his

Mistress was the most influential exhibit of its variety. And more Restoration poets learned something from him than from any other. Among the least expected debtors we may name two. Marvell certainly had profited from reading *The Mistress* (1647) and Rochester knew, as well as Dryden, how to make use of Cowley. To his essay *Of Liberty* Cowley added some verses translated from Martial, which contained these lines:

> *If there be Man (ye Gods) I ought to hate,*
> *Dependance and Attendance be his Fate,*
> *Still let him busie be, and in a Croud,*
> *And very much a Slave, and very proud.*

Perhaps this sounds to us more like Rochester than Cowley, even before we find it in a fragmentary letter by Rochester:

'I'le tell you were that mans soule plac't in a body fitt for it, hee were a dogg, that could count any thing a benifitt obtain'd with flattery, feare, & service,

> *Is there a man yee gods, whome I doe hate*
> *Dependance and Attendance bee his fate*
> *Lett him bee busy still & in a crowde*
> *And very much a slave & very proude.'*

This use certainly suggests, beyond the improvement in numbers, the author of *A Satyr against Mankind*.

Dr. Johnson, in his *Life of Cowley*, has generalized Cowley's wit in a summarizing passage usually overlooked in favour of the more striking remarks about Metaphysical wit: 'He makes no selection of words, nor seeks any neatness of phrase: he has no elegances either lucky or elaborate; as his endeavours were rather to impress sentences upon the understanding than images on the fancy, he has few epithets, and those scattered without peculiar propriety or nice adaptation.' This unexpected statement is best interpreted by another passage: 'One of the great sources of poetical delight is description, or the power of presenting pictures to the mind. Cowley gives inferences instead of images, and shews not what may be supposed to have been seen, but what thoughts the sight might have suggested.' This explains the opposition of sentences and images in the preceding quotation, which might apply to Fulke Greville. Moreover, 'the grandeur of generality' may be lost in particularity: 'Thus all the power of description is destroyed by a scrupulous enumeration; and the force of metaphors is lost, when the mind by the mention of particulars is turned more upon the original than the secondary sense, more upon that from which the illustration is drawn than that to which it is applied.' For Johnson this defect is augmented in Cowley by his 'great comprehension of knowledge and great fertility of fancy'. And Hobbes said that the latter depended upon the former. But one can also say that Cowley's metaphorical wit occasionally gave way to a Neo-classical kind of generality in which an epithet is coupled with an abstraction.

Yet Dr. Johnson allowed the Metaphysicals to be admired in one area: 'where scholastick speculation can be properly admitted, their copiousness and acuteness may justly be admired. What Cowley has written upon Hope shews an unequalled fertility of invention'. Although 'Against Hope', which is in *The Mistress*, exhibits the fancy for which Cowley was so much admired, it also approaches the general terms which Dr. Johnson admired in the grandeur of generality. And it must have taught Marvell and Rochester something about the use of abstractions in poetry, if it did not actually inspire 'Upon Nothing' or even 'The Definition of Love'.

In 'Against Hope' Cowley shows how hope at first defies definition by opposites or antithesis, but later is more responsive to his metaphorical wit. Thus he begins in this vein:

> *Hope, whose weak Being ruin'd is,*
> *Alike if it succeed, and if it miss;*
> *Whom Good or Ill does equally confound,*
> *And both the Horns of Fates Dilemma wound.*

Both his contraries and his metaphors, however, are organized by the stanzas so as to present hope in successive characters—as shadow, as wastrel, as cheater, and as dupe. In the last character it approaches the most obvious form of wit:

Brother of Fear, more gaily clad!
The merr'ier Fool o' th' two, yet quite as Mad:
Sire of Repentance, Child of fond Desire!
That blow'st the Chymicks, and the Lovers fire!
  Leading them still insensibly' on
  By the strange withcraft of Anon!
By Thee the one does changing Nature through
  Her endless Labyrinths pursue,
And th' other chases Woman, whilst She goes
More ways and turns than hunted Nature knows.

To the witty simile this adds a note of the melancholy Cowley, which is best heard in his English version of the limping elegiac metre, as in 'The Motto':

What shall I do to be for ever known,
  And make the Age to come my own?
I shall like Beasts or Common People die,
  Unless you write my Elegy;
Whilst others Great by being Born are grown,
  Their Mothers Labour, not their own.

As Dr. Johnson says, this 'ought to be inscribed *To my muse*, for want of which the second couplet is without reference'. Of course the point is that his muse must do for him what birth may do for others, but here not without a pun on 'labour'. This couplet adaptation of the classical elegiac may be compared with its use by Jonson in *The Forest*, 'To Sir Robert Wroth', and by Marvell in 'The Mower against Gardens'.

It was also in *The Mistress* that Cowley expressed the wish that came to dominate his life, In a rural retreat he would escape the vices of the city, which he suggests by witty parallels:

Pride and Ambition here,
Only in far fetcht Metaphors appear;
Here nought but winds can hurtful Murmurs scatter,
And nought but Eccho flatter.

The Gods, when they descended, hither
From Heav'n did always chuse their way;
And therefore we may boldly say,
That 'tis the way too thither.

Marvell gives his version of 'The Wish' in 'The Garden', and in both poems woman threatens to spoil the retreat, but for different reasons, though both turn on solitude.

Even in the elegy Cowley could exhibit the kind of wit that we find in Marvell's 'Garden'. For example, 'On the Death of Mr Crashaw' praises his dedication of poetry to divine subjects and then contrasts the work of more worldly poets. Despite Donne as Carew praised him,

Still the old Heathen Gods in Numbers dwell,
The Heav'nliest thing on Earth still keeps up Hell.
Nor have we yet quite purg'd the Christian Land;
Still Idols here, like Calves at Bethel stand.
And though Pans Death long since all Oracles broke,
Yet still in Rhyme the Fiend Apollo spoke:
Nay with the worst of Heathen dotage We
(Vain men!) the Monster Woman Deifie;
Find Stars, and tye our Fates there in a Face,
And Paradise in them by whom we lost it, place.
What different faults corrupt our Muses thus?
Wanton as Girls, as old Wives, Fabulous!

Thus poetry ought to shake off both the dotage into which it has fallen and the wit inherited by the sons of Ben. And to prove it, Cowley gives every line some ingenious turn deriving from other sources of wit.

In the *Davideis* Cowley's description of Heaven is a kind of antithesis to his Hell, but much more indebted to paradoxical Ovidian wit. Its infinity is less amenable to definition:

Above the subtle Foldings of the Sky,
Above the well-set Orbs soft Harmony,
Above those pretty Lamps that gild the Night,
There is a Place o'erflown with hallow'd Light;

Where Heav'n, as if it left it self behind,
Is stretcht out far, nor its own Bounds can find:
Here peaceful Flames swell up the sacred Place,
Nor can the Glory contain it self in th'endless Space.

It is on this last line that Cowley writes the note which Dr. Johnson quotes on representative versification: 'I am sorry that it is
necessary to admonish the most part of readers, that it is not by
negligence that this verse is so loose, long, and, as it were, vast;
it is to paint in the number the nature of the thing which it
describes.' It may be added that the nature of the thing here also
escapes in paradox.

In late Cowley, 'On the Queen's repairing Somerset-House',
his couplet can be seen turning more precisely in the path of Neo-
classical general terms:

Before my Gate a Street's broad Channel goes,
Which still with Waves of crouding People flows,
And ev'ry Day there passes by my Side,
Up to its Western Reach, the London Tide,
The Spring-Tides of the Term; my Front looks down
On all the Pride, and Business of the Town. . . .
    And here, behold, in a long bending Row,
How two joint Cities make one glorious Bow:
The Midst, the noblest Place, possess'd by me;
Best to be seen by all, and all o'ersee.
Which Way soe'er I turn my joyful Eye,
Here the great Court, there the rich Town, I spy;
On either Side dwells Safety and Delight;
Wealth on the Left, and Pow'r upon the Right.

But while these couplets are shaped by Ovidian turns they are
still touched by the pun; gone, however, are the hard metaphors
and particular terms. In short, propriety is more evident than ingenuity. And, as Dr. Johnson said, 'if he left versification yet
improvable, he left likewise from time to time such specimens of
excellence as enabled succeeding poets to improve it'. But it
remained for Dryden to give the syntax of Waller's couplet a
more natural order without sacrificing its antithetic rhetoric.

V

RESTORATION WIT

* I *

In theory Dryden owed much to Davenant, Hobbes, and Cowley, and not least to the problem which they left him—the regulation of wit. His career may be said to turn on this problem. He first saw it in these terms (*Preface to the Rival Ladies*): 'For imagination in a poet is a faculty so wild and lawless, that like an high-ranging spaniel, it must have clogs tied to it, lest it outrun the judgment.' The solution to this problem at first seemed to lie in metrics, in rhyme, or so he argued: 'But certainly, that which most regulates the fancy, and gives the judgment its busiest employment, is like to bring forth the richest and clearest thoughts.'

In the 'Preface to Annus Mirabilis' he asserts that 'the composition of all poems is, or ought to be, of wit', and then proceeds to discuss wit in the poet both as the faculty and as the product of imagination. The poet's imagination is then given a rhetorical analysis in terms of invention, disposition, and elocution, but disposition bears another name: 'the second is fancy, or the variation, deriving, or moulding, of that thought, as the judgment represents it proper to the subject'. This analysis elaborates the first description of imagination, 'which searches over all the memory for the species or ideas of those things which it designs to represent'. It will be noticed that judgment enters the process as the arbiter of propriety. The virtues of the imagination are related to the three functions: 'the quickness of the imagination is seen in the invention, the fertility in the fancy, and the accuracy in the expression'.

But the product of imagination is the centre of our interest, and

84

of this Dryden writes: '*Wit written* is that which is well defined, the happy result of thought, or product of imagination. But to proceed from wit, in the general notion of it, to the proper wit of an Heroic or Historical Poem, I judge it chiefly to consist in the delightful imagining of persons, actions, passions, or things. 'Tis not the jerk or sting of an epigram, nor the seeming contradiction of a poor antithesis (the delight of an ill-judging audience in a play of rhyme), nor the jingle of a more poor paronomasia; neither is it so much the morality of a grave sentence, affected by Lucan, but more sparingly used by Virgil; but it is some lively and apt description, dressed in such colours of speech, that it sets before your eyes the absent object, as perfectly, and more delightfully than nature.' This is Dr. Johnson's 'power of presenting pictures to the mind'. For Dryden in 1667 what is not considered the proper wit of the heroic mode is related to Lucan, but this rejection did not inhibit the authors of *The Rehearsal*. Dryden outmodes the wit of Davenant's young men, and goes beyond Cowley by rejecting antithesis, although he is talking about the heroic mode.

Since he has alluded to the dramatic, we may notice that 'the proper wit of dialogue' does not permit 'the study and choice of words' because it 'is supposed to be the effect of sudden thought; which, though it excludes not the quickness of wit in repartees, yet admits not a too curious election of words, too frequent allusions, or use of tropes, or, in fine, anything that shows remoteness of thought, or labour in the writer'. But the epic poet, who speaks mostly in his own person, is able 'to express his thoughts with all the graces of elocution, to write more figuratively, and to confess as well the labour as the force of his imagination'. Dryden makes the difference of genres important to the definition of wit.

Dryden begins his *Essay of Dramatic Poesy* (1668) by satirizing two styles of poetic wit: 'I ask you, if one of them does not perpetually pay us with clenches upon words, and a certain clownish kind of raillery? if now and then he does not offer at a catachresis or Clevelandism, wresting and torturing a word into another meaning.' The other presents an opposite style; it 'neither has wit in it, nor seems to have it': 'He affects plainness, to cover his want of imagination: when he writes the serious way, the highest flight

of his fancy is some miserable antithesis, or seeming contradiction; and in the comic he is still reaching at some thin conceit,
the ghost of a jest, and that too flies before him, never to be
caught.' The first style is again satirized in *Mac Flecknoe*, and the
second is reprehended here in both the comic and the serious way,
in which antithesis becomes a flight.

Later the Clevelandism is further defined when it is said of 'our
satyrist, Cleveland' that 'to express a thing hard and unnaturally,
is his new way of elocution. 'Tis true, no poet but may sometimes
use a catachresis. . . . But to do this always, and never be able to
write a line without it, though it may be admired by some few
pedants, will not pass upon those who know that wit is best con-
veyed to us in the most easy language . . . but we cannot read a
verse of Cleveland's without making a face at it, as if every word
were a pill to swallow: he gives us many times a hard nut to break
our teeth, without a kernel for our pains. So that there is this
difference betwixt his Satires and doctor Donne's; that the one
gives us deep thoughts in common language, though rough
cadence; the other gives us common thoughts in abstruse words.'
Hobbes had objected to scholastic terms or hard words as 'palpable darkness', and Dryden finds this fault in the hard metaphors of Cleveland rather than of Donne.

But Dryden exempts some of the more Neo-classical examples
of Cleveland's wit:

'"Tis true, in some places his wit is independent of his words, as
in that of the *Rebel Scot*:

> *Had* Cain *been* Scot, *God would have chang'd his doom;*
> *Not forc'd him wander, but confin'd him home.*

Si sic omnia dixisset! This is wit in all languages: 'tis like Mercury,
never to be lost or killed:—and so that other—

> *For beauty, like white powder, makes no noise,*
> *And yet the silent hypocrite destroys.*

You see, the last line is highly metaphorical, but it is so soft and
gentle, that it does not shock us as we read it.'

Although this example from *Rupertismus* is highly metaphorical, it is not catachrestic, but this satire exhibits more of 'Wit's Superfetation' of learning. However, Dryden now regarded Cleveland's wit as primarily verbal excess.

Dryden was loath to admit that Jonson had wit. In his *Essay* he was not far from Butler's words on the wit of *A Small Poet*: 'For bar him the Imitation of something he has read, and he has no Image in his Thoughts.' In 1671 he said: 'That Ben Jonson's plays were pleasant, he must want reason who denies: but that pleasantness was not properly wit, or the sharpness of conceit, but the natural imitation of folly,' which is rather an effect of observation and judgment. Despite his fondness for 'the ornaments of wit', Dryden concludes: 'Yet, as Mr. Cowley (who had a greater portion of it than any man I know) tells us in his *Character of Wit*, rather than all wit, let there be none.' And he deplores 'the superfluity and waste of wit' in Fletcher and Shakespeare. But in 1672, after conceding that Jonson 'always writ properly, and as the character required', he declared: 'and I will not contest farther with my friends who call that wit: it being very certain, that even folly itself, well represented, is wit in a larger signification; and that there is fancy, as well as judgment, in it, though not so much or noble: because all poetry being imitation, that of folly is a lower exercise of fancy, though perhaps as difficult as the other'. If Shadwell forced Dryden to this admission, he did not introduce the author of *An Essay of Dramatic Poesy* to this 'larger signification' of wit. Moreover, Hobbes had limited imagination by binding it to the imitation of nature. But in surrendering his distinction between wit as imitation and wit as 'sharpness of conceit' Dryden was raising other problems for himself.

In 1667 when Sprat made his inventory and appraisal of wit in *The History of the Royal Society* (III, xxxv), he may have been influenced by Cowley's statement that 'Fancy, does but Dream, when it is not guided by Sensible Objects.' Certainly the best wit in Sprat's view derives from the fancy when so guided, or when the mind of man is oriented towards Bacon's objective Nature and the imagination limited by this Nature. He undertakes to show the wits and writers how knowledge of 'the Works of

Nature' will provide them with 'an inexhaustible Treasure of Fancy and Invention'. Hobbes had urged knowledge as the way to wealth of fancy and had related it to nature. This is the background for Sprat's premise: 'To this purpose I must premise, that it is requir'd in the best, and most delightful *Wit*; that it be founded on such images which are generally known, and are able to bring a strong, and a sensible impression on the *mind*.' Thus Sprat limits the figurative imagination by the criteria which he sets up for wit or the products of wit.

Sprat then enumerates 'the several subjects from which it has been raised in all Times'. But he knows that wit has had a wider basis than is found in his premise, and so he says: 'In all these, where there may be a resemblance of one thing to another, as there may be in all, there is a sufficient Foundation for *Wit*.' He then offers the reason for his inventory: 'This in all its kinds has its increases, heights, and decays, as well as all other human things: Let us then examin what Parts of it are already exhausted, and what remain new, and untouch'd, and are still likely to be farther advanc'd.' This leads him into a Baconian inventory of wit.

Mythology is now rejected for a reason which goes beyond that of Sir Thomas Browne: 'Truth is never so well express'd or amplify'd, as by those Ornaments which are True and Real in themselves.'

'The Wit which is raised from Civil Histories, and the Customs of Countries, is solid and lasting: The Similitudes it affords are substantial, and equal to the minds of men, being drawn from themselves and their own actions.'

'The Manners, and Tempers, and Extravagances of men are a standing and eternal foundation of Wit: This if it be gathered from particular Observations, is called Humor: And the more particular they are, they are still the pleasanter.' When he relates humour to English drama, he reflects his quarrel with Sorbière.

'The Wit that may be borrowed from the *Bible* is magnificent, and as all the other Treasures of Knowledge it contains, inexhaustible. This may be used and allowed without any danger of

prophaness.' He then offers a defence of its use, and charges that
'the very Enthusiasts themselves, who are wont to start at such
Wit as Atheistical, are more guilty of its excesses than any other
sort of men'. For whenever they apply Scripture 'to themselves,
their Enemies, or their Country, though they call it the mind of
God, yet it is nothing else but Scripture comparison and Similitude.'

Then Sprat discounts the wit derived from subjects most
definitely disabled by his premise: 'The Sciences of mens Brains
are none of the best Materials for this kind of Wit. Very few have
happily succeeded in Logical, Metaphysical, Grammatical, nay
even scarce in Mathematical Comparisons; and the reason is,
because they are most of them conversant about things removed
from the Senses, and so cannot surprise the *fancy* with very
obvious, or quick, or sensible delights.' This outlaws the Metaphysical mode rather more definitely than did Hobbes.

Lastly Sprat, like Bacon, speaks of the areas that are capable of
improvement: 'The Wit that is founded on the Arts of mens
hands, is masculine and durable: It consists of Images that are
generally observed, and such visible things which are familiar to
mens minds. This therefore I will reckon as the first sort, which is
still improvable by the advancement of Experiments. And to this
I will add the Works of Nature, which are one of the best and
most fruitful Soils for the growth of Wit. It is apparent, that the
defect of the Antients in Natural Knowledge did also streighten
their Fancies: Those few things which they knew, they used so
much, and applied so often, that they even almost wore them
away by their using.'

From this state of things Experiments will rescue the poets:
'The Comparisons which these may afford will be intelligible to
all, because they proceed from things that enter into all mens
Senses. These will make the most vigorous impressions on mens
Fancies, because they do even touch their Eyes, and are nearest
to their Nature.' Bacon is cited as an example of the wonderful
advantage that may be derived from them: 'This excellent Writer
was abundantly recompenced for his Noble Labours in that
Philosophy, by a vast Treasure of admirable Imaginations which

it afforded him, wherewith to express and adorn his thoughts about other matters.'

Thus Bacon's Nature becomes the most promising source of wit, and Bacon himself 'one of the first and most artificial Managers of this way of Wit'. Sprat addresses the wits and writers as an unfriendly group, and so appeals to the *railleurs* not to make the New Philosophy ridiculous because it is new. For he was not recommending a source of ridicule or wit to 'tickle the fancy'. But he was arguing that wit should be more and more subdued to the nature of things, and limited in fancy by Bacon's empirical world.

John Eachard is also concerned with the use of wit in *The Grounds & Occasions of the Contempt of the Clergy* (1670). But no particular philosophy is a ground for this contempt: 'Neither shall I here examin which Philosophy, the old or new, makes the best Sermons: It is hard to say that Exhortations can be to no purpose, if the Preacher believes that the Earth turns round: Or, that his Reproofs can take no effect, unless he will suppose a *Vacuum*. There has been good Sermons, no question, made in the dayes of *Materia Prima*, and *Occult Qualities*: And there is, doubtless, still good Discourses now under the Reign of *Atoms*.' Yet the Puritans are said in Walker's *Sufferings of the Clergy* to have ejected a clergyman 'because he was a scandalous eater of custard'. But neither philosophy nor the wit derived from it was a matter of indifference to Sprat. And we have only to recall Donne's 'Nocturnal upon St. Lucy's Day' or Marvell's 'Horatian Ode' to realize that this passage applies to poems as well as to sermons.

In 'An Essay of Heroic Plays' Dryden returns in 1672 to the subject of heroic style or wit. Lucan offers an example of what it should not be, because he 'crowded sentences together, was too full of points, and too often offered at somewhat which had more of the sting of an epigram, than of the dignity and state of an heroic poem'. This is the epigrammatic mode that Dryden has reprehended before. But Dryden also deplores Lucan's neglect of 'those enthusiastic parts of poetry, which compose the most noble parts' of other epic poets.

Here he finds himself in opposition to the defenders of *Gondi-*

bert and their limitation of the imagination. Thus he argues: 'And if any man object the improbabilities of a spirit appearing, or of a palace raised by magic; I boldly answer him, that an heroic poet is not tied to a bare representation of what is true, or exceeding probable; but that he may let himself loose to visionary objects, and to the representation of such things as depending not on sense, and therefore not to be comprehended by knowledge, may give him a freer scope for imagination. 'Tis enough that, in all ages and religions, the greatest part of mankind have believed the power of magic, and that there are spirits or spectres which have appeared. This, I say, is foundation enough for poetry.' And thus Dryden escapes the limitation by appealing to Hobbes' articles of belief. And on this subject he thinks poets better than philosophers: 'For their speculations on this subject are wholly poetical; they have only their fancy for their guide.' He might have added that even Hobbes had agreed that where knowledge was lacking or uncertain the poet had to depend on fancy. This passage helps us to understand Hobbes better, and to relate Sprat's limitation of wit to Hobbes' limitation of the imagination.

Dryden, however, tries to accommodate his argument even to the letter of Hobbes: 'Some men think they have raised a great argument against the use of spectres and magic in heroic poetry, by saying they are unnatural; but whether they or I believe there are such things, is not material; 'tis enough that, for aught we know, they may be in Nature; and whatever is, or may be, is not properly unnatural.' He rejects Cowley for another reason: 'Neither am I much concerned at Mr. Cowley's verses before *Gondibert* (though his authority is almost sacred to me): 'tis true, he has resembled the epic poetry to a fantastic fairy-land; but he has contradicted himself by his own example.'

In 1675 in his 'Preface to Homer' Hobbes again had occasion to speak of fancy as a virtue in the heroic poem: 'A fourth is in the Elevation of Fancie, which is generally taken for the greatest praise of Heroique Poetry; and is so, when governed by discretion. For men more generally affect and admire Fancie than they do either Judgment, or Reason, or Memory, or any other intellectual Vertue; and for the pleasantness of it, give to it alone the

name of Wit, accounting Reason and Judgment but a dull entertainment.' This should clarify his remarks in the *Leviathan*.
Among the ornaments of wit, however, he qualifies metaphor:
'but when they are sharp and extraordinary, they are not fit for an
Heroique Poet, nor for a publique consultation, but only for an
Accusation or Defence at the Bar'. Lucan is the great example of
'height of Fancie', but also the occasion for remarking that
'though it be the mark of a great Wit, yet it is fitter for a Rhetorician than a Poet, and rebelleth often against Discretion'. This
emphasizes the extent to which Hobbes now feels—and before
Dryden settles on propriety—that the virtues 'indeed in all
writings published, are comprehended all in this one word,
Discretion'. But this still does not equate judgment with wit in
poetry, nor represent general opinion. Yet another objection was
then being raised by Edward Phillips in his 'Preface to *Theatrum
Poetarum*': 'Wit, Ingenuity, and Learning in Verse, even Elegancy it self, though that comes neerest, are one thing, true
Native *Poetry* is another.'

Samuel Butler, Cowley, and *The Rehearsal* condemn the same
general excesses of wit, differing only in particulars. But Butler is
in some respects the most illuminating of the three. In his 'Character of a Quibbler' he comes to this conclusion: 'There are two
Sorts of Quibbling, the one with Words, and the other with
Sense, like the Rhetoricians *Figurae Dictionis & Figurae Sententiae*—The first is already cried down, and the other as yet
prevails; and is the only Elegance of our modern Poets, which
easy Judges call *Easiness*; but having nothing in it but *Easiness*,
and being never used by any lasting Wit, will in wiser Times fall
to nothing of itself.' On the modern wit we cannot be sure that
Butler was alluding to Dryden's praise of Waller in the 'Preface
to the Rival Ladies', but we do know that Dryden also spoke
against this wit. Butler develops the first kind of wit in his fullest
inventory of reprehensible wit, which is found in his 'Character
of a Small Poet'. In this character Butler definitely involves
Benlowes.

Butler's small poet 'calls a slovenly nasty Description *great
Nature*, and dull Flatness *strange Easiness*.' At least he knows the

popular concepts. But true wit is beyond him because 'Observation and Fancy, the Matter and Form of just Wit, are above his Philosophy.' It is not uninstructive to observe some of his substitutes.

Here are some of the more interesting examples. 'For *Similitudes*, he likes the hardest and most obscure best.' Now a commonplace remark. More to Dryden's taste is this: 'When he writes, he commonly steers the Sense of his Lines by the Rhime that is at the End of them.' And here is the Clevelandism: 'For *Metaphors*, he uses to chuse the hardest, and most far-fet that he can light upon —These are the Jewels of Eloquence, and therefore the harder they are, the more precious they must be.' They are described with Addison's 'mixt Wit'.

And this is mythology for Butler: 'There is no Art in the World so rich in Terms as Poetry; a whole Dictionary is scarce able to contain them: For there is hardly a Pond, a Sheep-walk, or a Gravel-pit in all Greece, but the antient Name of it is become a Term of Art in Poetry. By this means small Poets have such a Stock of able hard Words lying by them, as *Dryades*, *Hamadryades*, *Aonides*, *Fauni*, *Nymphae*, *Sylvani*, *&c.* that signify nothing at all; and such a World of pedantic Terms of the same Kind, as may serve to furnish all the new Inventions and *thorough-Reformations*, that can happen between this and Plato's great Year.' This is the pedantry of the small poet.

In quibbling with words the Small Poet imitates a celebrated figure: 'When he writes *Anagrams*, he uses to lay the Outsides of his Verses even (like a Bricklayer) by a Line of Rhime and Acrostic, and fill the Middle with Rubbish—In this he imitates Ben. Jonson, but in nothing else.' In this kind of wit Benlowes is a master: 'There is no Feat of Activity, nor Gambol of Wit, that ever was performed by Man, from him that vaults on *Pegasus*, to him that tumbles through the Hoop of an Anagram, but Benlows has got the Mastery in it, whether it be high-rope Wit, or low-rope Wit. He has all Sorts of *Echoes*, *Rebus's*, *Chronograms*, &c. besides *Carwitchets*, *Clenches*, and *Quibbles*—As for *Altars* and *Pyramids* in Poetry, he has out-done all Men that Way; for he has made a *Gridiron*, and a *Frying-Pan* in Verse, that, beside the

Likeness in Shape, the very Tone and Sound of the Words did perfectly represent the Noise, that is made by those Utensils, such as the old Poet called *sartago loquendi*.' Such a catalogue is not found again until Addison; the sound effects may allude to Cowley's remarks about representative verse.

Butler observes significantly: 'Some Critics are of Opinion, that Poets ought to apply themselves to the Imitation of *Nature*, and make a Conscience of digressing from her; but he is none of these.' His illustration of violating this principle reminds us of the one given by Hobbes: 'And therefore when they give a Character of any Thing or Person, it does commonly bear no more Proportion to the Subject, than the Fishes and Ships in a Map do to the Scale.' As we have seen, the small poet has other ideas about the relation of poetry to nature.

While Butler was criticizing the wit of a small poet, Obadiah Walker was making English some Italian doctrine that led to such excesses. This doctrine came from E. Tesauro's *Il Cannocchiale Aristotelico* (1654) and M. Pellegrini's *I Fonti dell' Ingegno* (1650), and is to be found in Walker's *Of Education*. Chapter XI of that work is a discourse of invention, with advice on how to cultivate the three faculties of Wit, Memory, and Judgment, drawn largely from Tesauro and Pellegrini. Following Tesauro he defines 'Wit, the actions whereof are *fancy*, or *invention*,' after the manner of Hobbes. Wit is the mother of both facetious and serious invention. Moreover, invention may be bettered by practice in many of the witty forms criticized by Butler. Walker illustrates the use of topics or places in invention by means of Tesauro's Bee in Amber, which was probably the origin of the poem used in the article on wit by Hudson and Ustick in the *Huntington Library Bulletin* (No. 8). This article employs Addison on wit, and Tesauro must have been known to Addison through Bouhours' *La Manière de bien penser dans les Ouvrages d'Esprit*.

On the subject of quibbling Butler also said in his *Note-Books*: 'There are two ways of Quibling, the one with words, and the other with Sense; Like the Figurae Dictionis, and Figurae Sententiae, in Rhetorique. The first is don by shewing Tricks with words of the Same Sound, but Different Senses: And the other by expressing of Sense by Contradiction, and Riddle. Of this Mr. Waller, was the first most copious Author, and had so infected our modern writers of Heroiques with it, that they can hardly write any other way, and if at any time they indeavour to do it, like Horses that are put out of their Pace, they presently fall naturally into it againe.' Thus Waller was the first, in Butler's view, to make this figure a habit or character of style, as Dryden thought Cleveland had made the catachresis. This is essentially the Ovidian rhetoric, and Dryden observes it in Persius as well as Lucan. In his notes to his translation of Persius's First Satire he remarks: 'Persius here names Antitheses, or seeming Contradictions; which in this place are meant for Rhetorical flourishes.' This place is translated in a way that points his note:

> *With periods, points, and tropes, he slurs his crimes:*
> *'He robb'd not, but he borrow'd from the poor;*
> *And took but with intention to restore.'*

Aubrey's remark on Butler in *Brief Lives* should also be recalled: 'He haz often sayd that way (e.g. Mr. Edmund Waller's) of quibling with sence will hereafter growe as much out of fashion and be as ridicule as quibling with words—quod N.B.' In Butler's way of thinking Waller should be an unsung villain of *The Rehearsal*. Contradiction is at the centre of poetic wit in the seventeenth century. In its pure form it becomes paradox in the first half of the century and antithesis in the second; that is, contraries are reconciled in the one, and opposed in the other.

Buckingham's *Rehearsal* (1672) chastises many of the excesses of wit that had been the object of criticism at least since Cowley. It is directed against 'the new kind of Wits'—'fellows that scorn to imitate Nature; but are given altogether to elevate and surprise'. No doubt Bayes is meant to be Dryden when he says: 'I despise your Johnson, and Beaumont, that borrowed all they writ from Nature: I am for fetching it purely out of my own fancie.' This is the way to elevation and surprise. As Bayes says, 'the chief Art in Poetry is to elevate your expectation, and then bring you off some extraordinary way'. In Act IV, Scene ii, we are given 'an Heroick Scene'. Its elements are itemized as antithesis, reasoning in verse, striking simile, far-fetched fancy, rant or bold flights, and verse. Most of them derive from the emphasis on fancy and the desire to elevate and surprise.

When Dryden conceded that Jonson had wit in a larger sense, he did not grant him much wit in the stricter sense of 'sharpness of conceit', which is the concern of our study. Rather he chided him for quibbling with words, 'then the mode of wit', or else for borrowing his wit. And in 1677 he made one more defence of heroic wit in his 'Apology for Heroic Poetry and Poetic Licence'. There Dryden is sensitive to the growing criticism of the 'flights of heroic poetry', and argues that 'Virgil and Horace, the severest writers of the severest age, have made frequent use of the hardest metaphors, and of the strongest hyperboles.' These are ways of moving the passions originally discovered by poets but now part of the art of rhetoric. Thus although 'the knowledge of Nature was the original rule', the tropes and figures of rhetoric derive from it. Thus Dryden makes a defence of catachreses and hyperboles in the rhetoric of the heroic style.

Of Poetic Licence, or that which separates poetry from prose, Dryden says: 'This, as to what regards the thought or imagination of a poet, consists in fiction: but then those thoughts must be expressed; and here arise two other branches of it; for if this licence be included in a single word, it admits of tropes; if in a sentence or proposition, of figures; both which are of a much larger extent, and more forcibly to be used in verse than prose.' This is the basis of wit or what Puttenham called 'figurative conveyance'.

Dryden again encounters the problem of the supernatural when poetry is defined as an imitation of nature. How, for example, 'are things quite out of nature' to be imaged? This he answers by means of Hobbes' 'compound imagination'. But what of things 'whereof we can have no notion'? Poets may be allowed the liberty of 'describing things which really exist not, if they are founded on popular belief'. Dryden goes beyond Hobbes in making this 'still an imitation, though of other men's fancies'.

In conclusion Dryden attempted to suggest 'a standing measure of their controversy' as he had in *An Essay of Dramatic Poesy*:

'From that which has been said, it may be collected, that the definition of Wit (which has been so often attempted, and ever unsuccessfully by many poets) is only this: that it is a propriety of thoughts and words; or, in other terms, thoughts and words elegantly adapted to the subject. If our critics will join issue on this definition, that we may *convenire in aliquo tertio*; if they will take it as a granted principle, it will be easy to put an end to this dispute.' Therefore, Dryden believes, 'all reasonable men will conclude it necessary, that sublime subjects ought to be adorned with the sublimest, and consequently often with the most figurative expressions'. But his concern with the imitation of Shakespeare—'his whole style is so pestered with figurative expressions, that it is as affected as it is obscure'—finally persuaded him of the need to reform our poetry by abating its poetic licence in favour of stricter standards of propriety.

And in the 'Dedication of the Aeneis' in 1697 he altered the ground of propriety from thing to audience, requiring general terms for a general audience. This rejection of the proper terms of art which he had espoused in the 'Preface to Annus Mirabilis' clearly rejected the special terms of earlier wit. Dryden's rejections derive from the increasing claims of judgment against fancy. His attitude towards Cowley illustrates this change.

* 2 *

The range of wit in this time is perhaps best represented by Marvell and Waller, who connect the Interregnum and the Restoration.

Serious feeling and light fancy or wit appear in varying proportions in Marvell's poems; seldom, if ever, alone, though some are predominantly serious or witty. The dialogue, for example, lends itself to the development of a double mood, and Marvell was ingenious in exploiting its possibilities. In 'Clorinda and Damon' a contrast of theme and mood is expressed and magnified by a common pastoralism. The dialogue opposes pagan and Christian feeling, and hence the common images have different meanings, different associations, for each speaker. The antithesis is finally resolved in terms of a transcendent or Christian Pan, in whose praise the lovers can unite. Marvell has his own way of sophisticating pastoral feeling without adulterating it, and this sets him off from the cruder ways of the Restoration. But not in his later satire.

Although the pastoral had always involved the contrast of simplicity and sophistication, the Restoration pastoral exploited the mixture of town and country, or set the naive and the sophisticated into mocking opposition. Marvell plays the love of woman and the love of nature against each other in 'The Garden'. The Restoration lyric exhibits the sophistication of pastoral feeling in many forms, but it is truly modish when the naive convention is used to give piquant form to the amorous themes of the Restoration. Dryden's songs alone will illustrate the variety of the adulteration of pastoral feeling in this time.

As an exhibition of wit Marvell's 'Dialogue between the Soul and Body' must have few rivals in its kind. If we put it with the preceding dialogue and 'Bermudas', we get some idea of the ingenuity with which Marvell could treat a religious theme. In 'Bermudas' nature manifests the providence of God by an imagery that vividly separates the kind from the unkind island. In this dialogue common themes are given some uncommon turns. The Soul speaks of the body as prison and the soul as slave; the Body responds with the tyranny of the soul; the Soul retorts as the victim of the body and its ills; the Body replies as the victim of the soul and its ills. And the Body is given four additional lines as the last word.

But what gives the poem its great wit is the way in which these arguments are exaggerated or distorted by Marvell's caricature image. This poem provides a striking illustration of its equivocal use. In *The Rehearsal Transpros'd* (1672) Marvell burlesques the elevation of Bayes (Parker) in his own conceit, because his reputation for wit has made him vain: 'But after he was stretch'd to such an height in his own fancy, that he could not look down from top to toe but his Eyes dazled at the Precipice of his Stature; there fell out, or in, another natural chance which push'd him headlong.' His downfall came when he found favour with the ladies.

Now observe how Marvell uses this same image to caricature the tyranny of the soul:

> *Oh, who shall me deliver whole*
> *From bonds of this tyrannic soul?*
> *Which, stretched upright, impales me so*
> *That mine own precipice I go;*
> *And warms and moves this needless frame,*
> *A fever could but do the same.*

Thus his caricature wit can be put to serious purpose; here it enables him to point the Body's last word:

> *What but a soul could have the wit*
> *To build me up for sin so fit?*

The geometrical variety of his caricature wit is transcended most brilliantly in 'A Definition of Love'. For example:

> *As Lines so Loves* oblique *may well*
> *Themselves in every Angle greet:*
> *But ours so truly* Parallel,
> *Though infinite can never meet.*

In *The Rehearsal Transpros'd* it appears thus: 'He had put all princes upon the rack to stretch them to his dimension. And, as a straight line continued grows a circle, he had given them so infinite a power, that it was extended into impotency.'

The caricature image achieves its widest emotional range in 'To his Coy Mistress'. And the simplest form of his equivocal wit, as in 'The Coronet', is described by this jibe at Parker: 'Nor did I ever see a quibble fetched at greater distance, or more cunningly carried.' Indeed, the similarity of Marvell's lyric and satiric wit makes him resemble Cleveland more than any other contemporary, but his control over his virtuosity belongs to a more assured art. This art is also evident in his earlier satire, like 'Flecknoe', but is later sacrificed to the lampooning standards of the Restoration.

Another form of witty dissimulation is to introduce seeming contradiction or equivocation into the feelings of a poem, rather obviously in 'Clorinda and Damon'. This is illustrated more subtly in Marvell's 'Nymph complaining for the Death of her Fawn'. This poem enfolds a song of experience within a song of innocence; conveys both a feeling of innocence and a feeling of innocence outraged. The Nymph's feeling for her fawn is complicated by her feeling for her lover, Sylvio—for man's cruelty. The fawn serves to objectify both the innocence and the betrayal of the nymph, which endows the relationship with a range of feeling beyond that appropriate to a pet. Thus the poem acquires a sophisticated naiveté; the play of fancy connects with a kind of feeling much more serious than its occasion would ordinarily provoke.

The feeling toward men appears to be motivated by the death of the fawn. It does not extend so far as to wish them ill, but heaven will not forget; there is no expiation for this death. Ambiguity is latent in 'wanton troopers' and in the lines,

In this warm life-blood, which doth part
From thine, and wound me to the heart.

'Unconstant Sylvio', the 'counterfeit', the original 'wanton', gave her the fawn before he deserted her. His words were full of ambiguity,

Said he, Look how your huntsman here
Hath taught a fawn to hunt his dear.

Henceforth the fawn is her life; the ambiguity of her feeling is expressed in the lines,

How could I less
Than love it? Oh, I cannot be
Unkind t'a beast that loveth me.

She considers the possibility of the gift becoming as false as the giver, but concludes.

Thy love was far more better then
The love of false and cruel men.

Then several paragraphs develop her relation to the fawn: it never ran away (like Sylvio); it loved her garden. Here white and red project images of innocence and passion, with stress on the virginal. This relation culminates in the fawn's saint-like death, which makes it worthy of Heaven's regard and justifies the beginning. The nymph collects its tears with hers, to put in Diana's shrine. The fawn goes to the Elysium of the faithful and pure, and the nymph is to follow. But first her 'unhappy statue' must be cut in marble to resemble Niobe (slain by Diana, who was never conquered by love) and the fawn of alabaster laid at her feet:

> For I would have thine image be
> White as I can, though not as thee.

The nymph is to be remembered not as a Diana, but as a Niobe.

Marvell's 'Coy Mistress', like Donne's 'Sun Rising', finds its controlling image in the sun. Their 'long love's day' runs from the Ganges to the Humber before it is translated into cosmic hyperbole, or the sun's chariot is felt to be pursuing them. The subordinate figures of time and space produce that wonderful ambivalent image of 'Deserts of vast eternity', which unites enough time and space, but is both desert and beyond time. The great expansion of time and space in the first stanza is followed by the great contraction of the second; from the macrocosm of love to the microcosm of death, from the ideal to the real. Therefore the conclusion: let us consume time rather than be consumed by it; let us concentrate our pleasures and tear them through the 'iron gates' of life rather than languish in the slow-jawed power of time; both are closing images. Fate has 'iron wedges' in 'The Definition of Love'. The 'ball' is a small image of the world, a reduction which can make the sun appear to run. Thus they may circumvent the liabilities of time and her 'quaint honour'.

'The Definition of Love' centres upon figures of space, not time and space as in the 'Coy Mistress'. It is Marvell's poem 'Against Hope'. His love is distinguished by its birth and object: 'it was begotten by despair' upon the impossibility of attainment. Despair becomes magnanimous because of its divine object, and also stronger than hope because more daring. Fate separates him

from his object, 'Where my extended soul is fixed', though extension belongs only to body. Fate is jealous of their perfect love and
opposes their union, for it threatens her tyranny:

> *And therefore her Decrees of Steel*
> *Us as the distant Poles have plac'd,*
> *(Though Loves whole World on us doth wheel)*
> *Not by themselves to be embrac'd.*

Unless the world is changed, unless its geometry is altered, union
is impossible in the imagery of separation:

> *As Lines so Loves* oblique *may well*
> *Themselves in every Angle greet:*
> *But ours so truly* Parallel,
> *Though infinite can never meet.*

So defined, the very perfection of their love makes union impossible. In the comparison 'oblique' is an ambiguity meaning
both diverging and deviating from a given line or course; such
morally 'oblique loves' may meet in angles or corners.

> *Therefore the Love which us doth bind,*
> *But Fate so enviously debars,*
> *Is the Conjunction of the Mind,*
> *And Opposition of the Stars.*

This astronomical conclusion defines their love as a spiritual
union but a physical opposition or separation. Hope would have
selected a lower object and thus fallen short of the nobleness of
despair.

Marvell's 'Garden', from one point of view, deals with the
theme of the active versus the contemplative life. But Marvell,
like Cowley, treats the garden as the ideal state, or the image of
the state from which man fell; it is his paradise lost. Ambition and
the sweat of the brow bring small rewards compared to those of
the garden. Only here quiet and innocence, or their 'sacred Plants',
are now to be found (and were originally lost). The feminine per-
sonifications make them parallel to the desires of men in the next
stanza, where the beauty of nature is praised above the beauty of

woman as an object of desire. After passion's heat it is love's best retreat, as the gods have shown. In the garden man is provided for without effort but with innocence: in body (nature's sweets come to him), in mind (the higher pleasure of thought), in soul (preparation for the 'longer flight'):

> *Such was that happy Garden-state,*
> *While Man there walk'd without a Mate.*

Such was the original Paradise where man lost quiet and innocence, such the original rivalry of woman and garden which destroyed solitude. The 'Dial new' is a replica of the original Garden; it is not the work of vice found in 'The Mower against Gardens'. Here there is none of 'passion's heat' or 'flame', but a milder sun that runs through a yearly dial of flowers and herbs, which reckon best the rewards of time—the 'sweet and wholesome Hours' of the original Garden. The development in depth of this poem is characteristic of Marvell's wit.

Waller's wit in the lyric sometimes exhibits a relation to the past rather than the future. In fact one of the lyrics which still represent him in anthologies is a case in point. 'On a Girdle' depends for its wit upon a basic figure included in the title; for 'girdle' is a particular form of the general figure, circle, which includes all the supporting metaphors.

> *That which her slender waist confin'd,*
> *Shall now my joyfull temples bind;*
> *No Monarch but would give his Crowne*
> *His Armes might doe what this has done.*
>
> *It is my Heavens extreamest Spheare,*
> *The pale which held the lovely Deare,*
> *My joy, my griefe, my hope, my Love,*
> *Doe all within this Circle move.*
>
> *A narrow compass, and yet there*
> *Dwells all that's good, and all that's faire:*
> *Give me but what this Ribbon ty'd,*
> *Take all the sun goes round beside.*

The first lines suggest the poet's laurel; the second, the supreme conquest of a monarch. The basic figure becomes or includes Crowne, Spheare, pale, Circle, compass, Ribbon. The poem develops by the hyperbolic extension of 'circle' into kinds, assisted by plays upon ambiguities like 'Armes' and 'Deare'. The final opposition of his 'Deare' to the world does not leave the sun much else to go round, but it does extend the initial failure of 'Armes'.

In short, we may say that this poem exhibits a Metaphysical method: the extension of a genus by species or a class by kinds. It is the process Dr. Johnson had in mind when he complained about Donne's 'Valediction: of weeping' that 'The tears of lovers are always of great poetical account; but Donne has extended them into worlds.' In Waller this is the 'conceit' in the attenuated form employed by the Caroline poets.

Waller's greatest triumph in the witty use of myth is no doubt 'The story of Phoebus and Daphne applyed'. This myth becomes his conceit, or Gascoigne's device, for the whole poem. First he establishes his parallel:

> *Thirsis a youth of the inspired train,*
> *Faire Sacharissa lov'd, but lov'd in vain;*
> *Like Phoebus sung, the no less amorous boy;*
> *Like Daphne, she as lovely and as coy.*

Then the chase is described:

> *With numbers, he the flying Nymph pursues,*
> *With numbers, such as Phoebus selfe might use;*

until he

> *Had reach'd the Nymph with his harmonious lay,*
> *Whom all his charmes could not incline to stay.*

Then the poem turns toward its epigrammatic point:

> *Yet what he sung in his immortall straine,*
> *Though unsuccessfull, was not sung in vaine,*
> *All but the Nymph that should redress his wrong,*
> *Attend his passion, and approve his song.*

But the climax of his chase and his ultimate likeness to Phoebus is withheld until the epigrammatic close:

> *Like Phoebus thus acquiring unsought praise,*
> *He catch'd at love, and fill'd his arm with bayes.*

No doubt Waller thought this the happiest and most rewarding way for a poet to lose his love. It is also the sort of wit for which he was admired, though we might prefer the quieter point of 'unsought'.

Other poets used this myth incidentally. Christopher Brooke had anticipated Waller's point in a compliment to William Browne:

> *And, when from Daphne's tree he plucks more bays,*
> *His Shepherd's Pipe may chant more heav'nly lays.*

Cowley used it for derogation in 'The Spring':

> *Dull Creatures! 'tis not without Cause that she,*
> *Who fled the God of wit, was made a Tree.*

Marvell used it for approbation in 'The Garden':

> *The Gods, that mortal Beauty chase,*
> *Still in a Tree did end their race.*
> *Apollo hunted Daphne so,*
> *Only that She might Laurel grow.*

But only Waller made mythology the chief source of his wit.

Waller's paradoxical wit, without mythological support, is exhibited in 'The Selfe Banished'.

> *It is not that I love you less,*
> *Than when before your feet I lay,*
> *But to prevent the sad increase*
> *Of hopeless love, I keep away.*

The next three stanzas develop the unsoundness of his reason for making the vow. Then why should he keep it?

But vow'd I have, and never must
Your banish'd servant trouble you;
For if I breake, you may mistrust
The vow I made to love you too.

His reason for keeping a futile vow ends with the surprise of reversal—so that she will not doubt another vow. Comparison with Donne's Song, 'Sweetest love, I do not goe', will expose the attenuated argument of Waller's lyric as it is subordinated to epigrammatic point. He has made wit 'easy' or both neat and polite.

Of course Samuel Butler held Waller responsible for one sort of quibbling, 'by expressing of Sense by Contradiction, and Riddle'. For example, this passage on the Scots in the *Panegyrick* on Cromwell ends in a pyrotechnical display:

They, that henceforth must be content to know,
No warmer Region than their Hills of Snow,
May blame the Sun, but must extoll your Grace,
Which in our Senate has allow'd them place;
Preferr'd by Conquest, happily o'erthrowne,
Falling they rise, to be with us made one;
So kinde Dictators made, when they came home,
Their vanquish'd Foes, free Citizens of Rome.

Marvell in his 'Horatian Ode' also gave Cromwell some of his best verse, but he treated the Scots less civilly than Waller.

Waller celebrates the prowess of Cromwell in a way that was enough to provoke Charles II, as it did; and largely by historical allusions or general metaphors. With much more striking imagery Marvell writes an apology for Cromwell as the instrument of fate. In the opening figure of power Cromwell is lightning, but this figure gives way to the falcon, which is under control. Finally, to maintain his destiny he must keep his virtue. Although Marvell achieved a more heroic vein than Waller, he did not venture to justify Cromwell in these provocative terms:

Your never failing Sword made War to cease,
And now you heale us with the arts of Peace,

Our minds with bounty, and with awe engage,
Invite affection, and restrain our rage:
Less pleasure take, brave minds in battles won,
Than in restoring such as are undon,
Tygers have courage, and the rugged Bear,
But man alone can, whom he conquers, spare.
To pardon willing, and to punish loath,
You strike with one hand, but you heal with both,
Lifting up all that prostrate lie, you grieve
You cannot make the dead again to live:
When Fate, or Error had our Age mis-led,
And o'er these Nations such confusion spred,
The onely cure which could from Heav'n come down,
Was so much Power and Clemency in one.

If Dryden made the art of these lines truly provocative in his portrait of Achitophel, he also gave them a more natural order.

It was on this sort of verse that Butler had commented: 'Of this Mr. Waller, was the first most copious Author, and has so infected our modern writers of Heroiques with it, that they can hardly write any other way, and if at any time they endeavour to do it, like Horses that are put out of their Pace, they presently fall naturally into it againe.' Waller, in short, was the first to make the 'expressing of Sense by Contradiction' a style, whether in the form of paradox or antithesis. Cowley, on the other hand, was famous for the variety of his wit; and hence Waller is a better norm for the reigning wit of the Restoration. The smoother, more balanced manner of Waller's later verse may be illustrated out 'Of the last Verses in the Book':

The Seas are quiet, when the Winds give o'er
So calm are we, when Passions are no more:
For then we know how vain it was to boast
Of fleeting Things, so certain to be lost.
Clouds of Affection from our younger Eyes
Conceal that emptiness, which Age descries.

Here no ingenuity challenges the reign of the general term and the general metaphor.

VI

AUGUSTAN WIT

* I *

What Dryden rejected as the proper wit of the heroic poem in 1667 he emphatically denies the dramatic poem in 1679. Not that this restriction is new, but it is more specific: 'There is yet another obstacle to be removed, which is pointed wit, and sentences affected out of season; these are nothing of kin to the violence of passion: no man is at leisure to make sentences and similes, when his soul is in an agony. I the rather name this fault, that it may serve to remind me of my former errors.' He has begun to see the error of his ways; possibly because *The Rehearsal* had jeered: 'you must ever make a *simile* when you are surprised; 'tis the new way of writing'.

Perhaps Shakespeare converted him: 'I will not say of so great a poet, that he distinguished not the blown puffy style from true sublimity; but I may venture to maintain, that the fury of his fancy often transported him beyond the bounds of judgment, either in coining of new words and phrases, or racking words which were in use, into the violence of a catachresis.' Now Shakespeare seems too figurative and even guilty of Clevelandism; now bombast joins antithesis as 'the delight of an ill-judging audience.' And Ovid is rebuked in the 'Preface to Ovid's Epistles' because 'he is frequently witty out of season; leaving the imitation of Nature, and the cooler dictates of his judgment, for the false applause of Fancy'.

In his 'Dedication of the Spanish Friar' in 1681 Dryden rejects his earlier wit even more decisively: 'A famous modern poet used to sacrifice every year a Statius to Virgil's *Manes*; and I have indignation enough to burn a *D'Amboys* annually, to the memory of Johnson. But now, My Lord, I am sensible, perhaps too late, that I have gone too far: for, I remember some verses of my own *Maximin* and *Almanzor*, which cry vengeance upon me for their extravagance, and which I wish heartily in the same fire with Statius and Chapman.' If we recall the *Essay of Dramatic Poesy* we may conclude that the balance is shifting from fancy to judgment and that the poet who represented judgment then is rising in esteem. The plea of the 'Apology for Heroic Poetry and Poetic Licence' is now modified in terms of its conclusion to a plea for poetic restraint: 'so, in the heightenings of Poetry, the strength and vehemence of figures should be suited to the occasion, the subject, and the persons. All beyond this is monstrous: 'tis out of Nature, 'tis an excrescence, and not a living part of Poetry.' Dryden is learning from the errors of his youth that 'an injudicious poet who aims at loftiness runs easily into the swelling puffy style, because it looks like greatness'.

But some 'Delilahs of the theatre' were still tempting in 1690 when he wrote the 'Preface to Don Sebastian': 'It is obvious to every understanding reader, that the most poetical parts, which are descriptions, images, similitudes and moral sentences, are those which of necessity were to be pared away, when the body was swollen into too large a bulk for the representation of the stage.' Even Addison, however, entertained this view of 'figurative conveyance', although he was careful of propriety. In his 'Essay on Virgil's Georgics' in 1697 he finds that its subject permits 'those beautiful descriptions and images which are the spirit and life of Poetry'. Hence instead of direct expression the poet turns to indirect expression, developing that 'which had the most surprise, and by consequence the most delight in it'. Addison observes that 'to suggest a truth indirectly' pleases because it allows the mind to make its own discoveries, 'to apprehend an Idea that draws a whole train after it'.

In 1692 William Walsh made a significant statement about wit in his Preface to *Letters and Poems, Amorous and Gallant*. Speaking of the amorous verses, he says: 'Those who are conversant with the Writings of the Ancients, will observe a great difference between what they and the Moderns have publish'd upon this Subject. The Occasions upon which the Poems of the former are written, are such as happen to every Man almost that is in Love; and the Thoughts such, as are natural for every Man in Love to think. The Moderns, on the other hand, have sought out for Occasions that none meet with but themselves, and fill their Verses with Thoughts that are surprising and glittering, but not tender, passionate, or natural to a Man in Love.' This may reflect the quarrel of the Ancients and Moderns, but the propriety to Nature involves the end of such verses: 'And that I take not to be the getting of Fame or Admiration from the World, but the obtaining the Love of their Mistress; and the best way I conceive to make her love you, is to convince her that you love her. Now this certainly is not to be done by forc'd Conceits, far-fetch'd Similes, and shining Points; but by a true and lively Representation of the Pains and Thoughts attending such a Passion.' Obviously Walsh is a pragmatist and a rhetorician. After comparing Petrarch very unfavourably with the Ancients, he explains: 'I have chosen to mention Petrarch only, as being by much the most famous of all the Moderns who have written Love-verses: And it is, indeed, the great Reputation which he has gotten, that has given Encouragement to this false sort of Wit in the World.'

But Walsh wants to do right by the love verses of the English: 'Never was there a more copious Fancy or greater reach of Wit than what appears in Dr. Donne; nothing can be more gallant or gentle than the Poems of Mr. Waller; nothing more gay or sprightly than those of Sir John Suckling; and nothing fuller of Variety and Learning than Mr. Cowley's. However, it may be observ'd, that among all these, that Softness, Tenderness, and Violence of Passion, which the Ancients thought most proper for Love-verses, is wanting; and at the same time that we must allow Dr. Donne to have been a very great Wit; Mr. Waller a very gallant Writer; Sir John Suckling a very gay one, and Mr. Cowley a great Genius; yet methinks I can hardly fancy any one of them to have been a very great Lover.' Thus the 'knowing Walsh', with an eye to gallantry, reduces the effectiveness of modern love verses.

Dryden was now in a responsive mood for such remarks, and they seem to have provoked him to revise, in 1693, his earlier remarks about Donne: 'He affects the metaphysics, not only in his satires, but in his amorous verses, where nature only should reign; and perplexes the minds of the fair sex with nice speculations of philosophy, when he should engage their hearts, and entertain them with the softnesses of love.' Thus Dryden opposes nature to the wit of learning, and we may recall that Sprat had outmoded metaphysics as a source of wit.

Now Dryden becomes critical of Cowley and selective in his work: 'In this (if I may be pardoned for so bold a truth) Mr. Cowley has copied him to a fault; so great a one, in my opinion, that it throws his *Mistress* infinitely below his Pindarics and his latter compositions, which are undoubtedly the best of his poems, and the most correct.' His rejection of Cowley's earlier work in favour of his later work is significant, not least because it is made on the basis of correctness. Earlier, in the 'Preface to Sylvae', Dryden had said that one should not imitate a poet 'wherein either his thoughts are improper to his subject, or his expressions unworthy of his thoughts, or the turn of both is unharmonious'. For both Walsh and Dryden propriety limits the area of metaphor proper to the subject.

But Walsh's Preface did not pass without an answer. Charles Gildon's *Miscellaneous Letters and Essays*, published in 1694, contains 'An Essay at a Vindication of the Love-Verses of Cowley and Waller, &c.' in answer to Walsh. He finds Walsh's charges 'too general to be of any Force', but objects that they hit the Ancients too, 'many of whose Subjects or Occasions, are far from happening to all Lovers'. And 'there are a great many very tender and soft Thoughts, and passionate Expressions in Cowley's *Mistress*' as well as in other Moderns. Moreover, ' *Thoughts natural to a Man in Love*, is an obscure Expression' and 'seems to level the Thoughts of all Mankind': 'If by Thoughts surprizing, and glittering he means extraordinary and uncommon, I'm apt to think he will allow them very natural to Mr. Cowley or Mr. Waller in any Circumstance. A Man that is us'd to a good Habit of thinking, cannot be without extraordinary

Thoughts, on what concerns him so near as the Heart of his Mistress.'

And, still arguing the grounds of propriety, he adds: 'Besides, 'tis not to be supposed, that the Verses written by Lovers are the Extempore Result of a sudden Gust of Passion, like the Inspirations of the Delphic Prophetess. . . . A Poetizing Lover, must be allow'd not to be absolutely out of his wits, and that 'tis possible for him to study, and consider what he says in so solemn a Manner to his Mistress.' And what he may study includes the efficacy of his expression: 'Similes, fine Thoughts, and shining Points, if they be just, and good, must certainly give a greater Idea of any Pain, than a bare and unpolished Rhime, without Beauty or Grace. This gives us a weak, or faint, an unmoving View of the Pain; That sets it close to us, magnifies and enlarges it.' But in trying to vindicate the love verses of Cowley and Waller, Gildon was arguing a lost cause in outmoded terms.

In the same year Addison proved himself more up to date in *An Account of the Greatest English Poets*. He found Cowley guilty of violating a precept of his own *Ode of Wit*: 'Thy Fault is only Wit in its excess.' Or in other words,

> *His Turns too closely on the Reader press:*
> *He more had pleas'd us, had he pleas'd us less.*

Thus Addison imitates the turn that Dryden called a 'boyism' in Ovid and that Butler called the 'expressing of sense by contradiction' in Waller. Yet for 'courtly Waller' he reserves this compliment:

> *But now my Muse a softer Strain rehearse,*
> *Turn ev'ry Line with Art, and smooth thy Verse.*

This is the kind of turn for which Waller was still praised, but Addison's own muse was not yet emancipated.

Atterbury's Preface to Waller's *Poems*, printed in 1690, gives the most detailed statement of his achievement as it was then received. Unlike Butler, who had described the antithetic mode of wit in Waller, Atterbury is concerned with the verse that embodied that mode. After praising Waller's diction, he asserts:

'We are no less beholden to Him for the new turn of Verse, which he brought in, and the improvement he made in our Numbers.' This 'new turn of Verse' gave form to the antithetic mode of wit. Waller's harmony is defined in opposition to the rough cadence of Donne which Dryden had pointed out in 1668. Waller corrected the faults of that verse: 'There was no distinction of parts, no regular stops, nothing for the ear to rest upon: but, as soon as the copy began, down it went, like a larum, incessantly; and the reader was sure to be out of breath, before he got to the end of it. So that really Verse in those days was but down-right prose, tag'd with rhymes.'

Carew saw other things in this verse, and Atterbury admits that 'Suckling and Carew, I must confess, wrote some few things smoothly enough.' However, Atterbury proceeds to itemize the improvements: 'Mr. Waller remov'd all these faults; brought in more polysyllables, and smoother measures; bound up His thoughts better; and in a cadence more agreeable to the nature of the Verse He wrote in: so that where-ever the natural stops of that were, He contriv'd the little breakings of His sense so as to fall in with them. And for that reason, since the stress of our Verse lies commonly upon the last syllable, you'll hardly ever find Him using a word of no force there.' This is a perceptive statement of how Waller made 'the emphasis of sound coincide with that of sense', or made his antithetic wit pattern his verse, and his verse outline his wit so that rhyme became an instrument of point.

Dryden began this appraisal of Waller in his early essays, and in 1697 in the 'Dedication of the Aeneis' he again comments on the effect of monosyllables: 'for it seldom happens but a monosyllable line turns verse to prose; and even that prose is rugged and unharmonious. Philarchus, I remember, taxes Balzac for placing twenty monosyllables in file, without one dissyllable betwixt them.' Many of the faults that were corrected by Waller will be found in Dr. Johnson's analysis of Cowley's verse.

And Dryden once pointed to the most artificial development of this kind of verse. In 1685 he said in his 'Preface to Sylvae': 'All the versification and little variety of Claudian is included within the compass of four or five lines, and then he begins again in the same tenor; perpetually closing his sense at the end of a verse, and that verse commonly which they call golden, or two substantives and two adjectives, with a verb betwixt them to keep the peace.' Here prosody and rhetoric coincide. In our time this kind of verse has been criticized as the most stilted and padded form of Augustan couplet, especially by Saintsbury. But a school-book of Dryden's time, Charles Hoole's *New Discovery of the old Art of Teaching Schoole*, puts it into another context: 'They should often also vie amongst themselves, and strive who can make the best *Anagrams, Epigrams, Epitaphes, Epithalamia, Eclogues, Acrostics,* and *golden verses,* English, Latine, Greek, and Hebrew.' Some of these exercises are to be found among the bad forms of obsolete wit in Addison's *Spectator* papers on wit, but the golden verse itself became something like an archetype of the Augustan couplet, and its balance was animated by antithetic wit.

When Pope wrote to William Walsh in 1706 on the niceties of English verse, he related smoothness and variety of versification to the pause. Moreover, he drew his illustrations from Waller; his examples were these:

At the fifth.
> *Where'er thy navy | spreads her canvass wings,*

At the fourth.
> *Homage to thee | and peace to all she brings.*

At the sixth.
> *Like tracks of leverets | in morning snow.*

He observes that the pause 'at the fifth runs quicker', and is less monotonous if continued beyond three lines. Whether to admit the Hiatus between adjoining vowels is also important, and depends upon which offends the ear more, hiatus or elision.

The first two examples come from the first couplet of 'To the King on his Navy':

> *Where'er thy Navy spreads her canvass wings,*
> *Homage to thee, and peace to all she brings:*
> *The French and Spaniard, when thy Flags appear,*
> *Forget their hatred, and consent to fear.*

The wit of the characteristic rhetoric in the last line turns on the pointed ambiguity of 'consent', meaning both yield and agree to fear. The last example is from the poem, 'Of a Tree cut in Paper':

> *Fair hand! that can on virgin paper write,*
> *Yet from the stain of ink, preserve it white:*
> *Whose travel o'er that silver field does show,*
> *Like tracks of leverets in morning snow.*

Here the wit lies chiefly in the unexpected resemblance. But both passages illustrate what Atterbury described and what Pope admired in the versification of Waller.

Dryden's concern with wit in *Mac Flecknoe* is obvious, but his conception of the proper style for satire is also related to wit. In his 'Discourse concerning the Origin and Progress of Satire' (1693) he asks, 'Would not Donne's *Satires*, which abound with so much wit, appear more charming, if he had taken care of his words, and of his numbers?'[1] These defects and Dryden's taste for the heroic dictate his aims in satire. The mock-heroic appeals to him because its mixed tones afford him a dual satisfaction. Observe his comment on Tassoni's *Secchia Rapita*: 'The words are stately, the numbers smooth, the turn both of thoughts and words is happy. The first six lines of the stanza seem majestical and severe; but the two last turn them all into a pleasant ridicule.' His conception becomes clearer as he considers Boileau's *Lutrin*: 'He writes it in the French heroic verse, and calls it an heroic poem; his subject is trivial, but his verse is noble. I doubt not but he had Virgil in his eye, for we find many admirable imitations of him, and some parodies.'

Dryden's parallel, however, is misleading: 'as Virgil in his fourth Georgic, of the Bees, perpetually raises the lowness of his subject, by the loftiness of his words'. For satire, and especially the mock-heroic, one should read 'magnifies' for 'raises', unless

---

[1] This reputation pursued Donne into the eighteenth century in John Brown's 'Essay on Satire':

> *'Twas then plain Donne in honest vengeance rose,*
> *His Wit harmonious, tho' his Rhyme was prose:*
> *He 'midst an Age of Puns and Pedants wrote*
> *With genuine sense, and Roman strength of thought.*

one wants to defeat his end. But Dryden concludes: 'Here is the majesty of the heroic, finely mixed with the venom of the other; and raising the delight which otherwise would be flat and vulgar, by the sublimity of the expression.' This only magnifies his error and explains the occasional ambiguity in his mock-heroics. The fault lies in the impurity of his motivation in this kind of satire: the mock-heroic cannot yield a pure satisfaction to the heroic taste. For, as he says, the heroic is then mixed with the venom of satire. The separation of these dual satisfactions appears at its widest in *Absalom and Achitophel*.

Dryden felt that Hudibrastics lacked dignity of style: 'And besides, the double rhyme, (a necessary companion of burlesque writing,) is not so proper for manly satire; for it turns earnest too much to jest, and gives us a boyish kind of pleasure.' Butler should have left to others 'the excrescence of a word of two or three syllables in the close. 'Tis, indeed, below so great a master to make use of such a little instrument. But his good sense is perpetually shining through all he writes. . . . We pass through the levity of his rhyme, and are immediately carried into some admirable useful thought.' For Addison these double rhymes are a kind of false wit, even in Butler: 'I am afraid that great Numbers of those who admire the incomparable *Hudibras*, do it more on account of these Doggerel Rhymes than of the Parts that really deserve Admiration.' Yet Dryden well knew the value of this instrument for pointing wit, for bringing opposites together by a like sound, even ridiculous oppositions by double sounds, as in the famous character of Buckingham as Zimri 'drinking—thinking'. Of course Butler carried ingenuity in rhymes and hard words to its supreme achievements in such forms of wit. Yet Atterbury felt that Waller had taught the couplet how to use its rhymes.

But Waller's influence took another turn when Sir George Mackenzie asked Dryden why he did not imitate in his verses the turns on words and thoughts of Waller and Denham. This, says Dryden in his 'Discourse concerning Satire', happened 'about twenty years ago', or around 1673. Then he tells us, 'I looked over the darling of my youth, the famous Cowley; there I found, instead of them, the points of wit, and quirks of epigram, even in the *Davideis*, an heroic poem, which is of an opposite nature to those puerilities; but no elegant turns either on the word or on the thought.' But he did find them in Spenser, whom he thought, when he was boy, 'a mean poet, in comparison of Sylvester's *Dubartas*.' And he found that 'Virgil and Ovid are the two principal fountains of them in Latin poetry.' In 1718 Anthony Blackwall defines them in his *Introduction to the Classics* as follows: 'The most charming *Repetitions* are those, whereby the principal Words in a Sentence, either the same in Sound, or Signification, are repeated with such Advantage and Improvement, as raises a new Thought, or gives a musical Cadence and Harmony to the Period. These in *English* are call'd fine *Turns*; and are either upon the Words only, or the Thought, or both.'

But turns are not quibbles, and theoretically should not be confused, as Dryden later finds them confused in Ovid, whom Walsh included among the ancient love poets who wrote naturally. Now Dryden gives a turn from Virgil, 'which I cannot say is absolutely on words, for the thought turns with them':

> *Cum subita incautum dementia cepit amantem;*
> *Ignoscenda quidem, scirent si ignoscere Manes.*

But 'surely to be forgiven, if Death knew forgiveness' involves no quibble on word or sense. The difference is not always that clear in Ovid. Indeed, Ovidian wit and rhetoric have their place in Cowley as well as Waller, but Dryden is now dividing Ovid's quibbles and turns between Cowley and Waller. In 1697, in his 'Dedication of the Aeneis', he is apologetic about turns in his translation, and says flatly, 'the Epic Poem is too stately to receive those little ornaments'. Although he repeats the Virgilian turn given above, he now makes Ovid its principal addict.

In his 'Preface to the Fables' Dryden's view undergoes further change. First, in translating Ovid he revises his judgment of Sandys; his verdict in 1693 was based on memory, as he said, 'for I never read him since I was a boy'. Now, in translating parts of Ovid, he says, 'which I hope I have translated closely enough, and given them the same turn of verse which they had in the original; and this, I may say, without vanity, is not the talent of every poet. He who has arrived the nearest to it, is the ingenious and learned Sandys, the best versifier of the former age.' Now thoughts 'are to be measured only by their propriety'; and Ovid's 'are only glittering trifles, and so far from being witty, that in a serious poem they are nauseous, because they are unnatural'. For example, a man ready to die for love does not 'think of *inopem me copia fecit*', which Addison translated as, 'And too much Plenty makes me die for Want.' This is Butler's quibbling with sense, or 'expressing of sense by contradiction'.

It appears that Dryden now believed Ovid's turns on thought indistinguishable from what Butler called quibbling with sense. He says that Ovid 'would certainly have made Arcite witty on his deathbed: he had complained he was further off from possession, by being so near, and a thousand such boyisms, which Chaucer rejected as below the dignity of the subject'. He puts Ovid with Lucan and Martial, and then continues: 'As for the turn of words, in which Ovid particularly excels all poets, they are sometimes a fault, and sometimes a beauty, as they are used properly or improperly; but in strong passions always to be shunned, because passions are serious, and will admit no playing.' Thus the doctrine of decorum is narrowing the realm of wit as the Metaphysicals understood it.

Hence we should not be surprised by the rejection which follows: 'One of our late great poets is sunk in his reputation, because he could never forgive any conceit which came in his way; but swept like a drag-net, great and small. . . . All this proceeded not from any want of knowledge, but of judgment. Neither did he want that in discerning the beauties and faults of other poets, but only indulged himself in the luxury of writing; and perhaps knew it was a fault, but hoped the reader would not find it. For this reason, though he must always be thought a great poet, he is no longer esteemed a good writer.' And so Cowley goes out with the poets of the last age. His conceits include the quibbles of Ovid, and Dryden excused him with sympathy, but as if he recalled his earlier words in the 'Defence of an Essay': '*A great Wit's great work is to refuse*, as my worthy friend Sir John Berkenhead has ingeniously expressed it.' Perhaps he realized that he too had erred with Ovid.

Now Dryden had adopted in full the teaching of Hobbes: that the product of judgment is propriety (not poetic wit, as is often said); that the criterion of propriety is nature; and therefore that the guide and limit of fancy or imagination must be nature. This doctrine elevated Chaucer above Ovid and Cowley; in short, 'Chaucer followed Nature everywhere, but was never so bold to go beyond her.' Actually Hobbes said, 'beyond the conceived possibility of nature'. Waller has not yet sunk, like Cowley, because of his quibbling, as Butler predicted; but survives because of his 'turn of verse', to which the turns on words and thoughts contributed not a little. Indeed, Ovidian rhetoric replaces the Metaphysical in Neo-classical verse; it was fashioned in English by both Cowley and Waller, and hence was difficult for Dryden to escape.

The subject of wit, which occupies numbers 58–62 of *The Spectator*, was first approached by Addison in 1704 in his 'Notes on Ovid's *Metamorphoses*'. There too he uses Locke, but he does not suggest that something is lacking in Locke's definition of wit. Moreover, it should be recalled that Hobbes used fancy and judgment where Locke uses wit and judgment. After giving Locke's statement about wit, Addison continues in his *Notes*: 'Thus does True wit, as this incomparable Author observes, generally consist in the Likeness of Ideas, and is more or less Wit, as this likeness in Ideas is more surprising and unexpected. But as True wit is nothing else but a similitude in Ideas, so is False wit the similitude in Words, whether it lyes in the likeness of Letters only, as in Anagram and Acrostic; or of Syllables, as in Doggrel rhimes; or whole Words, as Puns, Echo's, and the like. Beside these two kinds of False and True wit, there is another of a middle nature, that has something of both in it. When in two Ideas that have some resemblance with each other, and are both expressed by the same word, we make use of the ambiguity of the word to speak that of one Idea included under it, which is proper to the other.' Again the example is the union of love and fire. The emphasis on surprise, however, is not Locke.

But Addison is more specific about one variety of mixed wit: if the poet 'finds any circumstance in his love contrary to the nature of fire, he calls his love a fire, and by joining this circumstance to it surprises his reader with a seeming contradiction'. Then he gives the reason for the length of this note: 'I should not have dwelt so long on this instance, had it not been so frequent in Ovid, who is the greatest admirer of this mixed wit of all the Ancients, as our Cowley is among the Moderns. Homer, Virgil, Horace, and the greatest Poets scorned it, as indeed it is only fit for Epigram and little copies of verses; one would wonder therefore how so sublime a genius as Milton could sometimes fall into it, in such a work as an Epic Poem.'

Earlier he had spoken of 'different Ideas compounded together' on a more substantial basis: 'This way of mixing two different Ideas together in one image, as it is a great surprise to the reader, is a great beauty in poetry, if there be sufficient ground for it in the nature of the thing that is described. The Latin Poets are very full of it, especially the worst of them, for the more correct use it but sparingly, as indeed the nature of things will seldom afford a just occasion for it.' Then he gives an example of the sort that produces seeming contradictions: 'Thus Claudian, having got a hollow ball of Chrystal with water in the midst of it for his subject, takes the advantage of considering the Chrystal as hard, stony, precious Water, and the Water as soft, fluid, imperfect Chrystal; and thus sports off above a dozen Epigrams, in setting his Words and Ideas at variance among one another.' Obviously Claudian is also adept at Ovidian wit.

Another variety of wit seems more definitely objectionable to Addison, and has greater interest for us. On the verse, 'And not my Chariot, but my Counsel take', he observes: 'Ovid's verse is *Consiliis non Curribus utere nostris.* This way of joining two such different Ideas as Chariot and Counsel to the same verb is mightily used by Ovid, but is a very low kind of wit, and has always in it a mixture of Pun, because the verb must be taken in a different sense when it is joined with one of the things, from what it has in conjunction with the other.' This way joins but does not mix or compound different ideas, and does it by ambiguity. It is often used by Cowley, but a famous example in Pope comes to mind:

> *Here thou, great Anna! whom three realms obey,*
> *Dost sometimes counsel take—and sometimes Tea.*

Addison would call this a quibble rather than a turn. But he did venture to say at this time: 'Ovid has more turns and repetitions in his words than any of the Latin Poets, which are always wonderfully easie and natural in him.' And these words remind us that Dryden paved the way for Addison not only by analysing turns but by finally rejecting them for serious poetry.

In the *Spectator* papers Addison makes a survey of all the forms of wit mentioned by Puttenham, Jonson, or Cowley. He distinguishes them by the categories set up in his 'Notes on Ovid', which utilize the categories by which Dryden discriminated turns. Among the makers of false wit Addison names Herbert, Sylvester, Butler, Andrewes, and Shakespeare. The last paper formulates the basic doctrine, and brings Locke's definition of wit closer to Hobbes' definition of fancy, because a resemblance of ideas without surprise is not wit: 'In order therefore that the Resemblance in the Ideas be Wit, it is necessary that the Ideas should not lie too near one another in the Nature of things; for where the Likeness is obvious, it gives no Surprize.' A good fancy, for Hobbes, had to see more than obvious likenesses. And Hoskins taught that the force of comparisons increased when the ideas did 'not lie too near one another in the Nature of things'.

Addison then makes a distinction that divides the old realm of wit: 'For this Reason, the Similitudes in Heroick Poets, who endeavour rather to fill the Mind with great Conceptions, than to divert it with such as are new and surprizing, have seldom any thing in them that can be called Wit.' Dr. Johnson extends this criticism to other poets in his *Life of Cowley*. In Addison wit is beginning to narrow its meaning to Dryden's new word 'witticism'. Perhaps Dryden himself prepared the way when he remarked of Ovid, in a passage which Addison quotes: 'Nature fails him; and, being forced to his old shift, he has recourse to witticism.' When Addison excludes wit from the heroic, he shows that it involves levity or some disproportion. The two now come together only in the mock-heroic, which capitalizes on disproportion.

But long before, in his 'Apology for Heroic Poetry', Dryden had resented having his own wit reduced to witticism: 'I have heard (says one of them) of anchovies dissolved in sauce; but never of an angel in hallelujahs. A mighty witticism! (if you will pardon a new word,) but there is some difference between a laugher and a critic.' If he had been guilty of poetic licence, still the image of wit and the image of imagination were not different things, except in burlesque. This witticism was made about Dryden's attempt to put *Paradise Lost* into dramatic form. At his best, however, Dryden can reduce Milton's spacious amplification to a poignant couplet:

> *In liquid Burnings, or on Dry to dwell,*
> *Is all the sad Variety of Hell.*

Here 'sad' is a loaded epithet intensifying 'little'; in fact the variety is only dry and liquid fire. The literal fades into its emotional value without becoming indefinitely suggestive; the metaphor is clearly limited by its context. This kind of neat intimation is essentially the Augustan form of poetic statement.

Addison now alters his list of those cited for 'mixt Wit': 'This kind of Wit is that which abounds in Cowley, more than in any Author that ever wrote. Mr. Waller has likewise a great deal of it. Mr. Dryden is very sparing in it. Milton had a Genius much above it.' If Addison now excuses Milton, he quarrels with Dryden's definition of wit because it is not a definition of wit in his narrower sense, although it does cover the 'great Conceptions' of his heroic poetry. When wit loses its surprise, it must please by its propriety, and this has 'its Foundation in the Nature of Things'. Addison is not consistent in approving the definition of wit by Bouhours, which also seeks the just through Nature and Truth.

Addison concludes his papers on wit by condemning the 'Gothick' taste which prefers Ovidian wit. Possibly he remembered that in the preceding year he had made Ned Softly admire the worst verses of Waller and 'the little Gothic ornaments of epigrammatical conceits, turns, points, and quibbles, which are so frequent in the most admired of our English poets'. These are the ornaments that Dryden considered repeatedly in connection with Ovid; they are included in the 'expressing of Sense by Contradiction and Riddle' which Butler thought Waller had stamped on the heroic couplet.

And at the very end Addison seems to realize that Locke's definition does not cover all wit. Although 'Resemblance and Congruity' may be the most fruitful source of wit, their opposites may also produce wit: 'For not only the Resemblance, but the Opposition of Ideas does very often produce Wit; as I could shew in several little Points, Turns, and Antitheses, that I may possibly enlarge upon in some future Speculation.' Antithesis is the only new term here, and it poses a question. Does he mean to distinguish it from the 'seeming Contradictions' of 'mixt Wit' which he associated with Ovid, Cowley, and Waller? Dryden did not distinguish them.

Some light on the problem may be found in Addison's 'Notes on Ovid'. But first let us recall Hoskins' treatment of antithesis, which was still being retailed by Thomas Blount's *Academie of Eloquence*. 'Comparison of contraries', says Hoskins, 'is the third and most flourishing way of comparison,' and it is found 'in the figure *contentio*, which is one of the instruments to aggravate by way of comparison.' In 1657 John Smith's *Mysterie of Rhetorique Unveiled* had added: '*Antithesis*, is also the illustration of a thing by its opposite.' Within limits Hoskins held that the force of a comparison increased as the unlikeness or inequality between the terms increased. Addison held that to be wit they 'should not lie too near one another in the Nature of things'; otherwise there would be no surprise. Obviously the terms or ideas in a comparison may vary in difference and in relationship: there are degrees in one and kinds in the other.

Addison, in his 'Notes on Ovid', always speaks of different ideas, but not always of the same relationship between them, except that some kind of resemblance is involved. For example, he finds characteristic of Ovid 'this way of joining two such different Ideas as Chariot and Counsel to the same verb.' Addison objects that these are joined by a pun on the verb 'take'. Except for the connecting likeness of 'being taken' they might have been mistaken for antithesis. Yet in another instance he speaks of 'two such different Ideas compounded together', not joined by an intermediate term. But 'this composition of different Ideas' may exploit the differences and multiply the surprise: 'In short, whenever the Poet feels any thing in this love that resembles something in fire, he carries on this agreement into a kind of allegory; but if, as in the preceding instances, he finds any circumstance in his love contrary to the nature of fire, he calls his love a fire, and by joining this circumstance to it surprises his reader with a seeming contradiction.' This is how the wit of contradiction develops within the wit of resemblance, which also depends upon some difference.

Hoskins calls this sort of thing *synoeciosis* or 'a composition of contraries', and a way to produce admiration in the hearer. In this kind of wit 'disagreeing Ideas are reconciled'; in antithesis they are opposed, and their opposition affects the verbal structure. In the composition of contraries (or different ideas) it is the composition that is surprising; in the opposition of contraries the surprise must derive from the contraries opposed. Hoskins would have said the aggravation or force rather than surprise of these kinds of comparison. In connecting Hoskins and Addison we realize how much the wit of the century emphasized resemblance in difference.

Thus Addison, like Sprat in his time, made an inventory and assessment of poetic wit. But perhaps we ought to conclude that Addison was no more successful than Dryden or Butler in stemming the wit that expresses 'sense by contradiction and riddle'. For the heirs of Waller refused to be 'put out of their Pace'. Ovidian wit and its rhetoric replaced the Metaphysical in Augustan verse. Pope often made use of the instruments that Addison condemned in Ovid, and once at Addison's expense—in the Character of Atticus:

View him with scornful, yet with jealous eyes,
And hate for arts that caus'd himself to rise;
Damn with faint praise, assent with civil leer,
And without sneering, teach the rest to sneer.

If the antithesis of the first line keeps the union of opposites from obvious consummation, the turn of the last line translates a negative into a positive sneer. The third line multiplies its antithetic elements until we have extremes meeting in a most uncivil leer. The examples of Ovidian wit that Dryden offers, such as 'plenty makes me poor' or 'further off from possession by being so near', are indeed 'boyisms' beside these; but they have the same formula: an opposite produces (or resembles) its opposite. Atticus does not suffer the crudity of this triplet:

His wit all see-saw, between that and this,
Now high, now low, now master up, now miss,
And he himself one vile Antithesis.

But we cannot conclude that Pope owed his finesse to a desire to take rhetorical revenge upon poor Addison.

* **2** *

The exemplary wit for this time is provided by Rochester and Dryden, who complement each other.

The emotional force of Rochester's poetry derives from an ethic of pain on the basis of which experience is explored by an agnostic wit. Only sense is certain, especially pain; this is often proved by the uncertainty of other knowledge. Pain is the test of true love in that moving song, 'An Age in her Embraces past'. When absence turns his soul into a shade, he amplifies the cause with ironic wit:

You wiser Men despise me not;
Whose Love-sick Fancy raves;
On Shades of Souls, and Heav'n knows what;
Short Ages live in Graves.

Whene'er those wounding Eyes, so full
Of Sweetness, you did see;
Had you not been profoundly dull,
You had gone mad like me.

Griefs are

The only Proof 'twixt them and me,
We love, and do not dream.

Indeed, torments have a religious efficacy, 'And make us blest at last'. In his paradoxical valediction, 'Absent from thee I languish still', pain is the only proof, the only test, for his infatuated mind:

Dear; *from thine Arms then let me fly,*
That my fantastick Mind may prove,
The Torments it deserves to try,
That tears my fixt Heart from my Love.

Finally, 'When wearied with a World of Woe', he prays that he may return to her bosom and 'contented there expire':

Lest once more wand'ring from that Heav'n,
I fall on some base Heart unblest;
Faithless to thee, false, unforgiven,
And lose my everlasting Rest.

Here the ambiguity of love and religion intensifies his feeling.

If pain tests the false, it also leads ultimately to the true. For all his agnostic wit, Rochester's best love poems are haunted by ideas of religion. This wit strikes its deepest note in his great paradox 'Upon Nothing'. It begins with the fear that is associated with his ethic of pain: '*Nothing!* thou elder Brother ev'n to Shade', who 'art alone, of Ending not afraid'. It resolves the issue of 'A Satyr against Mankind' with a Pascalian gambit:

Tho' Mysteries are barr'd from Laick Eyes,
And the Divine alone, with Warrant, pries
Into thy Bosom, where the Truth in private lies,

Yet this of thee the Wise may freely say,
Thou from the Virtuous nothing tak'st away,
And to be part with thee the Wicked wisely pray.

If the paradoxical wit of this century runs from poems like 'The Will' of Donne, which was mutilated by Sedley in 'The Lover's Will', through Cowley's 'Against Hope' to Rochester's 'Upon Nothing', it draws its varied power from a changing ethical basis rather than a new form of wit.

But 'The Maim'd Debauchee' employs a new form of wit. Thomas Rymer first called attention to Rochester's different uses of levity and seriousness: 'You wou'd take his *Monkey* for a Man of *Metaphysicks*; and his *Gondibert* he sends with all that Grimace to *demolish Windows*, or do some, the like *Important Mischief*.' The first use refers to his 'Satyr against Mankind' and the second to his 'Maim'd Debauchee' in the *Gondibert* stanza. The former opens by opposing the Monkey to the Man of Metaphysics:

> *Were I, who to my Cost already am,*
> *One of those strange, prodigious Creatures Man,*
> *A Spirit free, to chuse for my own Share,*
> *What sort of Flesh and Blood I pleas'd to wear,*
> *I'd be a Dog, a Monkey, or a Bear,*
> *Or any thing, but that vain Animal,*
> *Who is so proud of being Rational.*

The latter is described in terms of the mock-heroic. Just as Dryden inverts the usual valuation of sense and nonsense in 'Mac Flecknoe' and then treats this inversion in heroic style; so Rochester inverts the usual values of vice and virtue in 'The Maim'd Debauchee' and then treats this inversion in heroic style. He sends his Gondibert forth with a grimace that turns into virtue what the world regards as vice, just as Rochester in 'A Satyr against Mankind' ridicules reason in favour of sense, an inversion of the usual values.

'The Maim'd Debauchee' begins with an epic simile which Rochester proceeds to apply to the heroism of debauchery. It ends in contempt for the wisdom of impotence, which here too is associated with cowardice, as the lust for power is in 'A Satyr', or in Hobbes. Unlike the old soldier of 'Alexander's Feast', who fights all his battles over again, this is how he sees himself:

So when my Days of Impotence approach,
And I'me by Love and Wines unlucky chance,
Driv'n from the pleasing Billows of Debauch,
On the dull Shore of lazy Temperance.

My Pains at last some respite shall afford,
While I behold the Battels you maintain:
When Fleets of Glasses sail around the Board,
From whose Broad-Sides Volleys of Wit shall rain.

Even now this respite from pain is not the way to wisdom; rather
it is the negative side of his ethic—here best interpreted by his
letter to Henry Saville: 'Oh! That second Bottle (Harry!) is the
sincerest, wisest, and most impartial downright Friend we have;
tells us Truth of our selves, and forces us to speak Truths of
others; banishes Flattery from our Tongues, and Distrust from
our Hearts; sets us above the mean policy of Court-Prudence,
which makes us lie to one another all Day, for fear of being
Betray'd by each other at Night. And (before God) I believe the
errantest Villain breathing is honest as long as that Bottle lives,
and few of that Tribe dare venture upon him, at least among the
Courtiers and Statesmen.'

He urges others to the wars, and recalls his own exploits so as
to fire them to greater deeds:

With Tales like these I will such heat inspire,
As to important mischief shall incline;
I'le make him long some Ancient Church to fire,
And fear no lewdness they're call'd to by Wine.

The bravado of this important mischief finds its dimension in the
style, and leads to the mocking conclusion:

Thus Statesman-like I'le saucily impose,
And, safe from Danger, valiantly advise;
Shelter'd in impotence urge you to blows,
And, being good for nothing else, be wise.

Thus he turned another paradox on the fears which were con-
cealed behind the bravado that he epitomized in the famous paradox, 'For all Men, wou'd be *Cowards* if they durst'. But his

agnostic wit respected whatever made men honest—pain, fear,
wine—because it set them 'above the mean policy of Court-
Prudence'.

In *A Satyr against Mankind* the Monkey went on to nonplus the
Man of Metaphysics:

> *The senses are too gross; and he'll contrive*
> *A Sixth, to contradict the other Five:*
> *And before certain Instinct, will preferr*
> *Reason, which Fifty times for one does err—*
> *Reason, an* Ignis fatuus *of the Mind,*
> *Which leaves the Light of Nature, Sense, behind.*
> *Pathless, and dangerous, wand'ring ways it takes,*
> *Through Errour's fenny Bogs, and thorny Brakes:*
> *Whilst the misguided Follower climbs with Pain,*
> *Mountains of Whimsies, heapt in his own Brain,*
> *Stumbling from Thought to Thought, falls headlong down*
> *Into Doubt's boundless Sea, where like to drown*
> *Books bear him up a while, and make him try*
> *To swim with Bladders of Philosophy,*
> *In hopes still to o'ertake the skipping Light:*
> *The Vapour dances, in his dazzled sight,*
> *Till spent, it leaves him to Eternal Night.*
> *Then old Age, and Experience, hand in hand,*
> *Lead him to Death, and make him understand,*
> *After a Search so painful, and so long,*
> *That all his life he has been in the wrong.*

Reason and sense also complicated belief for Dryden, and this is
how he affected metaphysics in *The Hind and the Panther*, with
some of the same metaphorical wit:

> *What weight of ancient witness can prevail,*
> *If private reason hold the publick scale?*
> *But, gratious God, how well dost thou provide*
> *For erring judgments an unerring Guide!*
> *Thy throne is darkness in th'abyss of light,*
> *A blaze of glory that forbids the sight;*

O teach me to believe Thee thus conceal'd,
And search no farther than Thy self reveal'd . . .
My thoughtless youth was wing'd with vain desires,
My manhood, long misled by wandring fires,
Follow'd false lights; and when their glimps was gone,
My pride struck out new sparkles of her own. . . .
Can I believe eternal God could lye
Disguis'd in mortal mold and infancy?
That the great Maker of the world could dye?
And after that, trust my imperfect sense
Which calls in question his omnipotence?
Can I my reason to my faith compell,
And shall my sight, and touch, and taste rebell?
Superior faculties are set aside,
Shall their subservient organs be my guide?
Then let the moon usurp the rule of day,
And winking tapers shew the sun his way;
For what my senses can themselves perceive
I need no revelation to believe.

Thus Dryden answers for Rochester's 'formal Band and Beard', with old theological paradoxes put into rhetorical questions. These passages present the extreme answers then found to the ultimate question, which assumed a different form in Fulke Greville's 'Chorus Sacerdotum'. Their force depends largely upon the metaphorical wit with which they are amplified, and in this respect Rochester has the advantage, turning the wit of Donne into the Augustan mould.

Two of Dryden's satires, 'Mac Flecknoe' and 'Absalom and Achitophel', take their rise from the same problem: 'To settle the succession of the State'. In the comic satire, 'Nature is the best title to succession, but not in the serious satire, where nature has produced illegitimacy and complicated the problem. The narrative device is erected on this problem in both instances, but the heroic method differs in each.

In 'Absalom and Achitophel' the Biblical parallel imposes an elevated style which produces a mock-heroic effect when the

subject-matter will not support it, as in Charles's promiscuity or
in examples of petty vice rather than crimes. Otherwise the
elevated style sustains the heroic but inflates the villainous, as in
the monstrous Corah. It magnifies rather than diminishes crime,
but it still creates an effect of caricature. Of course the mock-
heroic disproportion may also be secured by inserting a deflating
term which produces a diminishing effect, as in parody. But
whether it be inflation or deflation, it still depends upon impropriety.

'Mac Flecknoe' is a purer example of the mock-heroic. The
inflation is applied solely for the purpose of deflation. A corona-
tion ceremony is used to ridicule an unworthy candidate; his
unworthiness is exaggerated by every requirement of the ceremony. The wit or surprise is produced by the impropriety or incongruity between style and subject-matter. But the reader is not
asked to change his attitude toward any part of the poem, or to
experience a mixed reaction as in 'Absalom and Achitophel'. Any
mixed effect is due wholly to the mixed tones created by the impropriety between vehicle and content.

The poem begins with a pretentious cliché about the law of
decay, which touches even nonsense and its absolute king. Among
his sons fit 'To reign, and wage immortal war with wit', only
Shadwell has no defect:

> *The rest to some faint meaning make pretense,*
> *But Sh— never deviates into sense.*

The wit, of course, lies in the normal impropriety of 'deviates'
to 'sense', which in this realm alone is not an impropriety. On the
other hand, 'a lucid interval' involves an ambiguity, that is, both
a moment of light or clarity and a moment of sanity.

Dryden's mock-heroic methods may be observed most effec-
tively in his use of parody or borrowed passages. When he locates
the throne near the dramatic Nursery, he borrows from Cowley:

> *Where their vast courts the mother-strumpets keep,*
> *And, undisturbed by watch, in silence sleep.*
> *Near these a Nursery erects its head,*
> *Where queens are form'd, and future heroes bred;*

Where unfledg'd actors learn to laugh and cry,
Where infant punks their tender voices try,
And little Maximins the gods defy.

In his 'Apology for Heroic Poetry and Poetic Licence' Dryden
had defended himself by citing a passage from Cowley's description of Hell in his *Davideis* (Book I):

Beneath the Dens where unfletcht Tempests lye,
And Infant Winds their tender Voices try . . .
Where their vast Court the Mother-waters keep,
And undisturb'd by Moons in Silence sleep. . . .

Dryden has urbanized Cowley's nature with a vengeance, and
this kind of deflation may have been suggested by the passage
which he defended against its detractors. He was rather proud of
this passage:

Seraph and Cherub, careless of their Charge,
And wanton, in full Ease now live at large;
Unguarded leave the Passes of the Sky,
And all dissolved in Hallelujahs lie.

But not so his critics. 'I have heard (says one of them) of anchovies
dissolved in sauce; but never of an angel in hallelujahs.' Perhaps
this comment opened his eyes to the possibilities of burlesquing
Cowley. At any rate, Cowley's Hell also suggested Shadwell's
'genuine night':

There is a Place deep, wondrous deep below,
Which genuine Night and Horror does o'erflow . . .
Here no dear Glimpse of the Sun's lovely Face
Strikes through the solid Darkness of the Place.

This is the darkness which has no 'lucid interval'.

For a line from Davenant's *Gondibert* Dryden alters nothing but
the context. In Davenant it is associated with reverence:

This to a structure led, long known to Fame,
And call'd, The Monument of vanish'd Minds.

In the realm of nonsense 'vanished' alters its meaning from 'departed' to 'non-existent'. A subtler turn is given another allusion:

> *His temples, last, with poppies were o'erspread,*
> *That nodding seem'd to consecrate his head.*

Annotations usually speak of Shadwell's addiction to opium, and we may allow poppies to be his own kind of laurel; but surely Shadwell is also 'consecrated' by his lapses, for Dryden knew Horace's remark that even Homer nodded (*dormitat*).

Among Dryden's many uses of Shadwell's literary work, we may notice his parody of Shadwell's definition of a humour:

> *A humor is the bias of the mind,*
> *By which with violence 'tis one way inclin'd:*
> *It makes our actions lean on one side still;*
> *And in all changes that way bends the will.*

In Dryden this becomes,

> *This is that boasted bias of thy mind,*
> *By which one way, to dulness, 'tis inclin'd,*
> *Which makes thy writings lean on one side still,*
> *And, in all changes, that way bends thy will.*

But Dryden immediately alludes to another way of 'arrogating Jonson's hostile name':

> *Nor let thy mountain-belly make pretense*
> *Of likeness; thine's a tympany of sense.*

This was a less accessible allusion to Jonson's poem, 'My Picture left in Scotland', but it must have stung its victim even more. And finally Shadwell is urged to cultivate 'acrostic land', a province of Addison's false wit lower than Clevelandism.

It should not be forgotten that Dryden could touch even the Pindaric ode with ironic wit. 'Alexander's Feast' affords some obvious examples. Recall this chorus:

With ravish'd Ears
The Monarch hears,
Assumes the God,
Affects to nod,
And seems to shake the Spheres.

If Alexander acquires some Restoration airs in this passage, he relapses into the old soldier in this one:

Sooth'd with the Sound, the King grew vain;
Fought all his Battails o'er again;
And thrice He routed all his Foes; and thrice
he slew the slain.

Perhaps Dryden's taste in satire finally touched his Pindarics, for 'here is the majesty of the heroic, finely mixed with the venom of the other'. At least his use of wit has not settled into the narrow mould of the mock-heroic, although his satire had already employed the long Pindaric line. But here we may parody Dryden on Timotheus and say that when

He rais'd a Mortal to the Skies,
He drew a Monarch down.

INDEX

INDEX

Hoskins, John, 14–15, 16–17, 22–3, 24–5, 28, 32, 47, 58, 60, 78, 121, 123, 124, (*Directions*, ed. H. H. Hudson)
Howell, James, 52
Hudson, Hoyt H., 94
Hurd, Richard, 18–19

Johnson, Samuel, 19, 23, 79–80, 81, 83, 85, 104, 113, 121
Jonson, Ben, 15–16, 23, 24, 26, 43, 45, 46, 47, 48–50, 51–2, 54, 56, 59, 60, 61–2, 74, 77–8, 81, 87, 93, 95, 96, 109, 121, 133

King, Henry, 51, 56–7, 73

Laforgue, Jules, 21
Landor, Walter Savage, 11
Leavis, F. R., 11
Legouis, Pierre, 27
Locke, John, 119, 121, 123
Longinus, 64
Lucan, 64, 65, 85, 90, 92, 95, 118

Mackenzie, Sir George, 116
Marino, Giovan Battista, 44
Marlowe, Christopher, 41
Martial, 61, 79, 118
Marvell, Andrew, 11, 21, 29, 57, 73, 78, 79, 80, 81, 82, 90, 97–103, 105, 106
Mayne, Jasper, 48, 64–5
Metaphysical Mode, 21, 23, 43, 49, 73, 74, 75, 79, 80, 86, 89, 104, 106, 111, 119, 124, 127, 129–30
Mill, Humphrey, 61
Milton, John, 14, 19, 29, 59, 65, 78, 120, 122
Morris, Corbyn, 22

Neo-classical Verse, 58–62, 112–14

Ovid, 52, 62, 63, 82, 83, 95, 108, 112, 117–21, 122–5
Ovidian Mode, 117–25

Parker, Samuel, 78, 98, 99
Pellegrini, Matteo, 94
Persius, 95
Petrarch, 44, 59, 110
Petrarchism, 20, 28, 33, 42, 44
Phillips, Edward, 92
Pindar, 43
Pindarics, 64, 70, 111, 133–4
Platonism, 34, 42

Pope, Alexander, 11, 44, 114–15, 121, 124–5
Praz, Mario, 13 n.
Puttenham, George, 12, 13, 14, 15, 19, 24, 45, 56, 96, 121

Quarles, Francis, 47
Querno, Camillo, 44
Quintilian, 13

Randolph, Thomas, 48
Rehearsal, The, 11, 85, 92, 95, 108
Reynolds, Henry, 47
Rochester, John Wilmot, Earl of, 11, 54, 79, 80, 125–30
Rymer, Thomas, 127

Saintsbury, George, 114
Sandys, George, 52, 53, 62, 117–18
Saville, Henry, 128
Sedley, Sir Charles, 127
Senecan Mode, 28, 71, 79–80
Shadwell, Thomas, 87, 132, 133
Shakespeare, William, 87, 108, 121
Sidney, Sir Philip, 13, 25–6, 28, 31–2, 44, 45, 64, 72
Smith, John, 22, 123
Spenser, Edmund, 59, 60, 117
Sprat, Thomas, 43, 58, 73, 87–90, 91, 124
Statius, 108, 109
Strada, Famianus, 44
Suckling, Sir John, 54–5, 110, 113
Sylvester, Joshua, 117, 121

Tasso, Torquato, 14, 46
Tassoni, Alessandro, 115
Tesauro, Emanuele, 94
Tillotson, John, 31
Tisdale, Roger, 16

Ustick, W. L., 94

Virgil, 62, 65, 85, 96, 108, 109, 115, 117, 120

Walker, John, 90
Walker, Obadiah, 63–4, 94
Waller, Edmund, 53–4, 55, 61, 70, 76, 83, 95, 97, 103–7, 110, 111, 112–13, 114–15, 116, 117, 119, 122, 123, 124
Walsh, William, 109–10, 111
Webster, John, 28
West, Richard, 48

136